Fa
Is
Substance

MW00608212

by

Percy Gutteridge

edited by Jim & Denise Kerwin
annotated by Jim Kerwin

FINEST OF THE WHEAT PUBLICATIONS

Faith Is Substance

Copyright © 2009, 2019
Finest of the Wheat Teaching Fellowship, Inc.
All rights reserved
Original edition published in 1975
by Bethesda Teaching Ministry

Third Edition

Most quotations from the Bible are taken
from the Authorized (King James) Version.
Scripture quotations marked NASB are taken
from the New American Standard Bible®,
copyright © 1960, 1962, 1963, 1968,
1971, 1972, 1973, 1975, 1977
by the Lockman Foundation
(www.Lockman.org).
Used by permission.

Cover design:
Murry Whiteman
(mwart.net)

More teaching resources by
Pastor Percy Gutteridge
and others are available at
FinestOfTheWheat.org

ISBN: 978-0988266766

Now faith is the substance
of things hoped for,
The evidence of things not seen....
Through faith we understand...

Hebrews 11:1,3

Table of Contents

Foreword to the 2019 Edition

P.H.P. ("PERCY") GUTTERIDGE was born 110 years ago on September 26, 1909. Only God Himself knew at the time that this newborn would grow up to be a truly Christ-like man, "full of the Holy Ghost and wisdom," a beloved pastor, Bible teacher, counselor, mentor, and friend to thousands of believers in many churches and denominations.

Percy was a much-loved and appreciated father in the Lord to me. We are ever aware as we grow older that our parents and mentors are growing older yet, and sometime soon will come a day when they are taken home to be with the Lord and we will lose their companionship, wisdom, counsel, and fellowship. This was in the back of my mind—Percy's eventual graduation to Glory and the consequent loss of his teaching ministry—when I wrote to him years ago, asking permission to reprint his material. Ever generous with what God had given him to share with others, Percy's response was unequivocal and encouraging:

> *...Most certainly use any of the Bethesda Teaching Ministry material as you see fit, and without further requests....*
>
> *Much love,*
> *Percy G.*

Since his handwritten note arrived, Pastor Gutteridge has gone on into the presence of Jesus, and received His "well done." My wife and I, bearing as we do in our hearts and spirits the fruit of the truths God sowed into us through Percy's ministry, have keenly felt the need to pass on Pastor's teaching to succeeding generations. Having Percy's written permission, we also sought the blessing of the surviving family. Thus free to proceed, in 2003 we began a labor of love by creating a Bible-teaching website on which we have made Pastor Gutteridge's material, starting with the full text of ***Faith Is Substance***, available free of charge to anyone interested. Over the years, that website has evolved into **FinestOfTheWheat.org**, a ministry of the non-profit Finest of the Wheat Teaching Fellowship, Inc. There the collection of Pastor's messages continues to grow, available in both text and audio format.

Percy often quoted the adage, *"A lie goes around the world while truth is still putting its boots on."* Certainly, given what passes for "truth" and "revelation" in so much of the Body of Christ today, that adage holds truer than ever, not the least when it comes to what is taught about faith. Many who knew Percy and were blessed with his teaching, counsel, and friendship would probably agree with my experience of the man, that, like Samuel of old, *"the Lord was with him, and did let none of his words fall to the ground"* (1 Samuel 3:19). That is especially true of the teaching in ***Faith Is Substance*** and its solid, uncompromising, "Holy Ghost common sense" presentation of real faith; the truths the book contains have laid a foundation in many believers which has stood the test of time and kept them from foolishness, fads, and misguided fanaticism.

It is with immense pleasure that we reissue ***Faith Is Substance*** and its everlasting truths to a new generation. May this new edition prove to be a blessing to those who knew and loved Pastor Gutteridge, to those seeking God's truth, and to all those who love the Lord Jesus Christ whom Pastor Gutteridge served so faithfully, humbly, and lovingly throughout his lifetime.

Rev. Jim Kerwin, M.A.
February 2019

Note: Profits from direct online sales of this book are being used to help fund Finest of the Wheat's missions trips to teach pastors and leaders in developing countries in Latin America and Eastern Europe.

Foreword to the Original 1975 Edition

BEHIND EVERY BOOK there is a life. The quality of that life determines the validity and vitality of the message presented! Only as the truth has first been translated into the breath and life of the writer can his pen become the instrument of power which will release the life of the reader for God's glory. This is particularly true as it relates to the grand and glorious theme of faith. This is not a topic for the novice, for its streams run deep and can only be reached by paying a price. Only men whose faith has been fire-tested in the crucible of experience have earned the right to share this treasure with others. True teachers of God minister from the wellsprings of life—both heavenly and earthly—as inspired by the Holy Spirit. There is great value in exposing our hearts and minds to their message, for they have been set in the Body of Christ for our edification.

It has been my privilege to know the Reverend Percy Gutteridge as a warm and personal friend for several years. He is one of God's gifted teachers who ministers from a life of a faith well-proven in experience. I have recognized the mantle of the Spirit upon his life not only from the fruit of his public teaching ministry, but from many profitable hours we have spent together in personal fellowship around the truth of God's Word. It was a most enriching experience which I realized needed to be shared in a more extensive way with the family of God. For this reason it is with personal joy and satisfaction that I write the foreword to this book, which in God's will I trust may be the first of many more.

—Dr. Robert C. Frost[1]*—*

1 Dr. Robert C. Frost was a leader in the Charismatic Movement in the United States. He authored such books as *Aglow with the Spirit, Set My Spirit Free, The Biology of the Holy Spirit, The Overflowing Life*, and *Our Heavenly Father.*

Introduction

THIS BOOK DOES NOT FLY THE FLAG of any denominational allegiance, nor is the writer prepared to break a lance on behalf of any sect or party. He has a deep concern to share with all truth-seekers what he has discovered through much spiritual travail in his sincere attempt to walk in the light, as it has been revealed to him. At the request of many thoughtful and loving people, this book has been penned so that there could be a more permanent form to the spoken word. Chief amongst these friendly people was Dr. Robert Frost who most graciously consented to write the foreword, but this does not put him under obligation to agree with the book's conclusions.

We will ask John Bunyan to be so kind as to lend us a part of his introduction to his immortal allegory, the *Pilgrim's Progress.* Here it is:

Thus I set pen to paper with delight,
And quickly had my thoughts in black and white,
For having now my method by the end,
Still as I pull'd it came; and so I penn'd
It down; until at last it came to be
For length and breadth, the bigness which you see...

...If that thou wilt not read, let it alone;
Some love the meat, some love to pick the bone...

...You see the ways the fisherman doth take
To catch the fish, what engines he doth make,
Yet fish there be that neither hook, nor line,

Nor snare, nor net, nor engine can make thine;
They must be groped for, and be tickled too,
Or they will not be catch'd whate'er you do....

Now may the Little Book a blessing be
To those that love this Little Book and me;
And may its buyer have no cause to say
His money is but lost or thrown away...

...Wouldst read thyself? O then, come hither
And lay my book, thy head and heart together.

—Percy Gutteridge—

FAITH
IS
SUBSTANCE

·1·
The Author and Foundation of Faith

Faith Is The *Substance*

FAITH IS NOT JUST THE FUSE of a spiritual explosion. It is more than the trigger to produce a sign and wonder. It is not just a necessary ingredient for a miracle. Faith is *substance*, in fact *the* substance that God created to be the pith and marrow of the true Christian life.

Faith was substance in Jack Mavros, one of God's hidden saints, very few of whom are known to the established Christian circles of earth; but "Grandpa Jack" was known in Heaven. He worked as a cobbler in his own small repair shop in North Hollywood, California.

A friend of mine was in his shop one day, when in blustered a motorcycle gang member in his typical black leather jacket. He hit the counter with a pair of shoes and yelled out, "Clean these, ol' man!" Grandpa Jack was not a cleaner of shoes, but a most able shoe repairer. He took up the shoes and cleaned and polished them beautifully, and then handed them back with his usual sweet smile.

"What's the take, ol' man?" asked the potential gangster.

Grandpa Jack looked puzzled. He said, "I'm sorry, but I don't understand. You see, I don't understand English too well. I'm a Greek."

"How much for the shoes?"

Now Grandpa Jack understood. "Oh, nothing!" he said. "Any time you are passing by, bring them in and I'll be delighted to do them for you!"

This drinking, swearing, drug-taking youth was stunned. He had gate-crashed into a different world, where faith in Jesus was not just a doctrine, or the repetition of scripture texts, or an occasional miracle, but *substance.* He went out of the shop in a daze. Perhaps for the first time in his life he had met with Jesus. The only words he could find to say were "Nut-case!", which he must have realized were completely inadequate to describe the situation.

Shortly after this, Grandpa Jack was called Home. They found him dead, on his knees. There came for him just such a summons as came for Mr. Standfast of the *Pilgrim's Progress* —*"The contents whereof were, that he must prepare for a change of life; for his Master was not willing that he should be so far from Him any longer."*

I also had the privilege of knowing Pastor George Hart of Glasgow, the founder of the India North-West Mission and the author of an amazing record of God's miraculous supply of his needs, *World Travel with the Living God.*[1] A friend of mine told me of this little revealing incident when Pastor Hart came as a guest to his home. It is a courteous custom in England to call a guest in the morning by taking him a cup of tea. Into Pastor Hart's bedroom he went with a cup of tea. He found him as he expected—praying. "Pastor," he said, "I have brought you a cup of tea." "Excuse me, Lord," said George Hart, "I'm going to have a cup of tea."

The Lord Jesus was real *to* these men and *in* these men. Their faith was the very substance of their lives. Because of this, the only true foundation, God could work miracles through them, for they were men of God. Shallow Christianity is as greatly entertained by fascinating accounts of miracles wrought by faith as the world is by magic or spiritualism or parapsychology, and Christians can be as ignorant as the world is of the faith which is the living substance of the "faith of the Son of God" (Galatians 2:20).

"Now faith is... substance" (Hebrews 11:1). *Hupostasis* is the Greek word, anglicized, translated *substance*, which means *that which stands under* or *substratum*. The word is used of title deeds which give assurance and confirmation of the fact of inheritance and ownership. Faith is not optimism, wishful thinking, nor looking on the bright side of things. It is sterling reality. Faith always works. It always produces. It is one of those everlasting principles, one of those laws or divine forces that are of the very foundation of the Kingdom of Heaven. **"Now abideth faith"** (1 Corinthians 13:13). So faith originated with God. He is the Almighty, Everlasting Believer from whom all faith originally proceeded. In His presence there can be neither doubts nor doubting. In Heaven, every living being of whatever order, rank, or quality fully believes God, and because of this has complete confidence and belief in the present—which is Faith; complete confidence and belief in the future—which is Hope; and complete confidence and belief in each other—which is Love.

Divine Faith—A Gift

All things that God has made bear the imprint of His fingers. God is a Trinity of three eternally distinct Persons in perfect unity; so all of His creation bears the stamp of His Tri-unity. Consider man—a most wonderful testimony to His creative skill: he is tripartite, a triple unity after the image of God. Man is dead if only a body; he is incomplete if but a soul; he is impersonal if only a spirit. As man is the image of his Creator, he has in faint measure what God has without degree.

Man *has* life; but God doesn't *have* life—He *is* Life! The Lord Jesus Christ, who is God manifest in the flesh, the visible image of the invisible God, proved His Deity by saying, "I am the Life" (John 14:6). The Nicene Creed[2] quite correctly has the Christian say, "I believe in the Holy Ghost, the Lord and Giver of Life." The Life of God is infinite and eternal in extent. Man is alive, but how limited, how circumscribed, how minute is his life in its degree.

God is also Love—unfathomable, everlasting, unmeasurable Love.

Stronger His love than death or hell;
Its riches are unsearchable;
The first-born sons of light
Desire in vain its depths to see;
They cannot tell the mystery,
The length and breadth and height.[3]

–Charles Wesley–

Man *has* love, but how limited it is! One of the highest forms of love we know on earth, in sacrificial quality, is that of a parent for a child—a mother's love, a father's love. "Can a woman forget her sucking child, that she should not have compassion on the son of her womb? *yea, they may forget,* yet will I not forget thee" (Isaiah 49:15).

Faith originated with God. Like His eternal life and His everlasting love, faith is of His essence, an essential quality of His nature. God exercises faith in an unlimited degree. It is revealed in the book of origins—Genesis. "And God said, 'Let there be...,' and there was..." (Genesis 1:3). This is faith. His Son is the Lamb slain from the foundation of the world (Revelation 13:8). Ever in the mind of God, from the beginning of the cosmos, was the intention, the unalterable design and belief that the Logos—the Everlasting Word—should be the One who would reconcile all things unto Himself. See how that Lamb, as God manifested in the flesh, representing the Father, exercised His divine faith—perfect faith: "Father... I knew that Thou hearest Me always" (John 11:41,42). All of His "I will's" are the demonstration of His faith; for although that handful of His disciples were so weak through the flesh that finally they all forsook Him and fled, yet the Word, strong in His almightiness and sustained by His divine faith, stood as an unassailable rock:

> *"I will make you to become fishers of men."*
>
> *Mark 1:17*

> *"I will build My Church."*
>
> *Matthew 16:18*

> *"I will come again and receive you unto Myself."*
>
> *John 14:3*

The faith that God has in absolute perfection He gave to man in limited measure when He created him in His own image; but since the fall of man, how much weaker now is the measure of faith man has.

One of the great errors of our present evangelical society is the confusion of the great fullness of original *divine* faith, the faith of God, with the human quality of faith resident in man. Human faith is limited; divine faith is unlimited. We confuse a steady confidence, a human optimism, a kindly trust, a genial benevolent glow of good will, with the all-conquering, almighty, ever-victorious faith of God. The faith of the Scriptures that subdued kingdoms, wrought righteousness, obtained promises, and many other things, is not the human quality, but the divine.

The apostles found that their faith was small and limited, so they petitioned the Master: "Lord, increase our faith" (Luke 17:5). Jesus replied, in effect: "You have no faith! If," said He, "ye had faith as a grain of mustard seed...." They had the human, but they needed the divine quality. All their human faith, although they exercised it together, would not move a pebble one inch; but one portion of divine faith—although only the size of a grain of mustard seed—has within it the potential to remove a mountain. Human faith is an inheritance, a part of our Adamic nature; but divine faith is a donation—"...**faith... not of yourselves**: it is the gift of God" (Ephesians 2:8).

Peter speaks of those who "**have obtained like precious faith with us**" (2 Peter 1:1). Consider a simple illustration. Human faith believes that, by a process of nature, sea water can be transformed into grape juice, but it is by a means far beyond man's ability to originally control or to effect. That is, by evaporation through the sun's heat and by the wind's conveyance of water vapor in the clouds, water from the oceans eventually reaches the vines and is transmuted by them into wine. Believing this, man prepares the soil, plants his vines, and so by faith, a *human* faith, eventually he receives the reward of his confidence. But it was by an act of *divine* faith that water was transformed by Jesus instantaneously into wine, better wine (John 2:1-11). Human faith believes that out there, in the great deep, there is a silver harvest to be gathered, and schemes and plans and labors to bring the fish in; but despite a night of toil it may be, at last, that nothing is taken (Luke 5:4-9). But, oh, the miracle of divine faith!

The Galilean fishers toil
All night and nothing take;
But Jesus comes—a wondrous spoil
Is lifted from the lake.

* * *

The night is dark, the surges fill
The bark, the wild winds roar;
But Jesus comes; and all is still–
The ship is at the shore.[4]

–Bishop Wordsworth–

All the stimulating pep-talks about turning faith loose really mean this: stir up and use your human faith, the Adamic faith that you have by nature. Notice the psychic[5] level on which it works and the kind of atmosphere it requires. Divine faith needs no atmosphere; it triumphs in spite of a hostile one. It bows adverse circumstances to its will. There is a power in the human quality of faith—but how faint, how limited it is. Compare, for example, a wayside scene in Palestine, and Jesus healing the sick, being moved with compassion by their sorrows, to the super-advertised, worked-up atmosphere and accompanying stage effects of some modern evangelistic healing services. One is the divine faith triumphing; the other is human faith being stimulated and the Lord in mercy healing a few sick folk. These simple peasants were not possessors of the new birth. The Holy Spirit was not yet given. But faith—a temporary faith—was quickened in them through the Living Word spoken, a faith produced by the presence of Jesus—the Word of God—and they were healed. Peter walked upon the water by this faith which came to him by the word of the Lord—"Come!" But the faith of the Son of God had no root in him; he was not yet born of the Spirit; his human faith could not sustain him to go on walking on the water, and he began to sink.

This precious gift of divine faith is an utter confidence in God, an assurance that what He says is true. When the life, as a consequence, is ordered in accord with this faith, it always produces a work. Otherwise, it is not a living, that is, a true, lasting and constant faith, but a dead one, says James (2:17).

Faith is believing what I know to be true; it is not an attempt to believe what I fear to be false. It is not the stultification of intelligence (which is credulity); it is superior to intelligence, yet it works in cooperation with it. Before this faith is divinely given, there must come a revelation of truth, that is, a word from God. "So then **faith cometh by hearing... the word of God**" (Romans 10:17). This is a personal and direct word given to an individual in whatever way God chooses, yet so that the one receiving it consciously realizes that the great and living God has spoken. This is one of the privileges of the Lord's sheep. "My sheep hear My voice" (John 10:27). Divine faith is always within the divine word, so "the sheep follow Him: for they know His voice" (John 10:4). The word of the Lord bringing with it its own quality of faith is not any word that anyone takes in his own will from the Scriptures, or from a promise box. If there were more waiting on the Lord, there would be more direct words from the Lord and more of the true life of faith being demonstrated in the midst of an unbelieving world. For faith can never be just a mental assent to a truism; faith must ever be translated into a corresponding positive action of the will to believe and do.

Unbelief and Non-Belief

Against positive faith stands the negative of **unbelief**. Unbelief is mental acceptance of untruth and a corresponding act of the will not to believe the truth. The untruth is accepted because in some way it is congenial to the carnal mind which is "not subject to the law of God, neither indeed can be" (Romans 8:7). "He did not many mighty works there **because of their unbelief**" (Matthew 13:58). The Scripture does not mean that He had not the power or was unable, but that under the circumstances no good would have been done by a display of the miraculous. Unbelief is a steady determination not to be convinced, whatever happens. It is revealed in the atheist who says to the believer in God, "You cannot prove to me the existence of God!" Already, you see, he has convinced himself that it is impossible to prove God's existence—"You *cannot* prove to me." Is there any value in trying to do so against such an attitude?

There is another state, not positive like faith or actively negative like unbelief; it is a *neutral* state which we may call "**non-belief**." It is not inclined to truth by its nature, like faith, nor is it antagonistic to truth by nature, like unbelief—although it may be in opposition through ignorance. Most people are *non*-believers, not *un*believers. The simple folk of Palestine, of whom Jesus said that they were like "sheep having no shepherd" (Matthew 9:36), were of this character, and so were swayed either way. If they were influenced by the Son of God, then they wanted to make Him king—even by force, if necessary. But when they were persuaded in the opposite direction by the priests and scribes and Pharisees, whom Jesus said were of their father, the devil, then they allowed Jesus to be crucified.

Acquiring Divine Faith

How does one acquire the divine quality of faith—the gift of God? The Most High uses as a bridge our inherited human faith: *"He that cometh to God must believe that He is"* (Hebrews 11:6). Then by our willing reception of an implanted incorruptible seed of the Word of God, given directly and personally by the incoming Holy Spirit, spiritual conception takes place. We are born from above: first birth in Adam has received second birth in the Son; old human birth has acquired new divine birth.

> *It is in the spiritual as in the natural life—some feel more, others less, but all experience some pangs and travails of soul, ere the Man Christ Jesus is formed within them, and brought forth and arrived unto the measure of His fullness Who filleth all in all. If God deals with thee in a more gentle way, yet so that a thorough work of conversion is effected in thine heart, thou oughtest to be exceedingly thankful. Or if he should lead thee through a longer wilderness than I have passed through, thou needest not complain. The more thou art humbled now, the more thou shalt be exalted hereafter. One taste of Christ's love in the heart will make amends for all. And if thou hast felt the powers of the world to come, and been made a partaker of the Holy Ghost, I know thou wilt rejoice, and give thanks for what God has done for my soul.*
>
> *George Whitefield, 1736 (Journals)*

This new birth is the impartation to us of an entirely new quality of life—"eternal life"—which is the very life of God. This God-given life miraculously changes a "goat" into a "sheep." The new sheep-life can never perish. It is divine; it lives forever. Because one of the qualities of the nature of God is the divine quality of faith, this most precious possession comes as part of the very nature of the new birth. So this faith is the gift of God —*"Not of yourselves, it is the gift of God"* (Ephesians 2:8).

But what treasures come with the gift of the Holy Spirit in new birth! With it all the various manifestations of the divine nature are given to man in limited measure—in seed form, but, nevertheless, in exactly the same divine quality as God has Himself. We receive the peace of God which flows like a river and which is beyond human understanding; the love of Christ which passes knowledge; the gift of immortality; the hope of God which stretches into the boundless eons of eternity; and the faith of God, steadfast and impregnable, which enables His children to begin to share "the exceeding greatness of His power to usward who believe" (Ephesians 1:19). All this in seed —not in fullness; the same in quality—not in quantity. It is not infinite in supply in us as it is in God. On earth, all living things grow to maturity and then begin to decline; but those who have the divine life will grow forever. It is a growth that goes on to infinity. His children are a perfect image of their Beloved, in their limited measure; but they will ever be reaching up towards the full stature of the Son of God. They will throughout all successive ages, all new dispensations, all other dimensions, throughout all eternity, whilst serving Him in the sphere of His appointing, ever be arriving at a new sphere of service and being prepared for yet further spheres; for "His servants shall serve Him" (Revelation 22:3).

Spirit of faith, come down,
Reveal the things of God,
And make to us the Godhead known,
And witness with the blood.
'Tis Thine the blood to apply,
And give us eyes to see;
Who did for every sinner die,
Hath surely died for me.

* * *

Inspire the living faith,
Which whosoe'er receives,
The witness in himself he hath,
And consciously believes;
The faith that conquers all,
And doth the mountains move,

And saves whoe'er on Jesus call,
And perfects them in love.[6]

–Charles Wesley–

ENDNOTES FOR CHAPTER 1

1. *World Travel with the Living God* by George Hart had a foreword by none other than J. Edwin Orr. It was published by Marshall, Morgan & Scott, Ltd. (London and Edinburgh). The date was not provided on the title page.

2. The Nicene Creed is one of the earliest statements of faith and correct belief. Adopted by a major church council which met in 325 A.D. in the city of Nicaea (hence the word *Nicene*), it was later revised by a church council meeting in Constantinople in 381 A.D. The creed is still recited in the liturgies of many denominations.

3. The quote is the second verse of Wesley's hymn ***O Love Divine, How Sweet Thou Art!***. The full text appears on page 178.

4. From Wordsworth's hymn ***The Galilean Fishers Toil***, included on page 179 in the appendix.

5. *Psychic*, as Pastor Gutteridge uses it here and elsewhere, refers to *the power of the mind*. The word is derived from the Greek *psuchē (ψυχή)*, the New Testament word usually translated into English as *soul*.

6. These are the first and fifth verses of Wesley's ***Spirit of Faith, Come Down***. All five verses appear in the appendix, beginning on page 181.

·2·
The Conditions of Faith

WHAT ARE THE CONDITIONS of faith? We do not mean, "What physical or soulish conditions are necessary to enable faith to work?" nor "How may we arrange the circumstances or how may we procure the right atmosphere by the use of soul-thrilling music or by drama or by the charming display of an extraordinary human personality?" We have tried to make it clear that the faith of the Scriptures is a *spiritual* faith, not a *psychic* one; it is ***the faith of God***. Therefore we are not concerned with outward atmosphere, but with *spiritual* conditions, that is, with the spirit of the man of faith.

We have already said that faith works in spite of contrary conditions. If that were not so, there would be no need of faith. Usually circumstances and conditions are against the victory of an act of faith. For example:

- **Noah**—by faith—built an ark, an unsinkable ship, to float in a worldwide storm of such titanic dimensions that it is beyond human thought even to conceive of it. No past or present shipyard could produce a ship to keep afloat through such a universal deluge (Genesis 6-8).

- **Abraham and Sarah** received miraculous ability—by faith—to produce a child, when every physiologically relevant fact shouted against their ability to do so (Hebrews 11:11-12).

- **Abraham**—by faith—was prepared to slay his son, burn him to ashes on an altar, and then expect to see his son rise from the ashes, phoenix-like, in newness of life, "from whence also he received him in a figure" (Hebrews 11:17-19).
- All the evidence was against human levitation in the days of **Enoch**. No one had ever risen from earth before. But—by faith—"Enoch was translated [taken up into the heavens]" (Hebrews 11:5), "for God took him" (Genesis 5:24).

Utter Helplessness: A Worm's-Eye View of Faith

The man of faith is **one who has felt his complete need of it**—one who has no confidence in the flesh. To whom does God promise that he shall be "a new sharp threshing instrument having teeth" that should "thresh the mountains, and beat them small, and make the hills as chaff"? To whom does He say, "Fear not"? He says it to "thou worm Jacob" (Isaiah 41:14,15). A worm is the most lowly thing on earth. It is a weak, despised, helpless thing—a prey to the mole which burrows for it in the earth, and a prey to the thrush which listens and watches for it above ground. It has no defenses against attack; it has no means of offense; it is a prey to fear. A worm has no voice to cry out for help; it has no eyes to see; it has no ears to hear; it is a trembling thing, sensitive to every vibration.

"Fear not," says the Living God to every weak, trembling Jacob, for these are the candidates for a living and triumphant faith. Jesus took our place; He calls *Himself* a worm:

"But I am a worm and no man;
a reproach of men and despised of the people."

— Psalm 22:6 —

These are the prophetic, messianic words inspired by the Holy Spirit. God says, to confirm this:

"Behold My servant, whom I uphold;
Mine elect, in whom My soul delighteth.
I have put My Spirit upon Him...
He shall not cry, nor lift up,
Nor cause His voice to be heard in the street.
A bruised reed He shall not break,
And the smoking flax[1] *shall He not quench."*

— Isaiah 42:1-3 —

Again He says, "Who is blind, but my Servant? or deaf, as my messenger that I sent?" (Isaiah 42:19).

But this is the faithful One who "shall not fail nor be discouraged, till He have set judgment in the earth" (Isaiah 42:4). He shall "open the blind eyes, to bring out the prisoners from the prison, and them that sit in darkness out of the prison house" (Isaiah 42:7). This One who made Himself a worm is the only One who is God's man of faith and God's man for the hour. Would you share in His triumph of faith? Then you must fulfill the conditions and be of His character.

The spirit of our evangelical age is contrary to this. We puff up, we inflate, we shout our loud advertisement of a man. We glory in education and human ability; we are ever alert to listen to the latest clever preacher, that we also might be amongst the knowledgeable, lest we should be considered ignorant. To what a pass we have come! No wonder true faith declines, and substitute faith is so often the order of the day. Listen again to the Holy Spirit speaking to the early Christians through Paul:

> [26]*For ye see your calling, brethren, how that not many wise men after the flesh, not many mighty, not many noble, are called:* [27]*But God hath chosen the foolish things of the world to confound the wise; and God hath chosen the weak things of the world to confound the things which are mighty;* [28]*And base things of the world, and things which are despised, hath God chosen, yea, and things which are not, to bring to nought things that are:* [29]*That no flesh should glory in His presence...* [31]*...as it is written, He that glorieth, let him glory in the Lord.*
>
> *1 Corinthians 1:26-29,31*

The Lord Jesus confirms this: "I thank Thee, O Father, Lord of heaven and earth, because Thou hast hid these things from the wise and prudent, and hast revealed them unto babes. Even so, Father: for so it seemed good in Thy sight" (Matthew 11:25,26). What God has hidden, no man can find. He has hidden from man His life, His truth, His faith, His love, His Son; all can come to us only by His unveiling, through direct personal revelation.

Spiritual Poverty

Associated with this condition of humility is that of poverty. What is spiritual poverty? What did Jesus mean when He said, "Blessed be ye poor: for yours is the Kingdom of God" (Luke 6:20)? True Christian poverty is not a physical condition, but a spiritual one. Matthew's equally inspired record of this beatitude includes two additional words: "Blessed are the poor *in spirit*" (Matthew 5:3). This makes it quite clear that the Lord is not saying that being poor of itself is the condition for being a possessor of the Kingdom of God, nor conversely, that one who has wealth is of necessity excluded from it; but that being poor or being rich must have the foundation of a Christ-like spirit. To be poor in this sense means that I own nothing; that all I have, little or much, I hold as a responsible steward of God; and that I am ready to dispense it how and when and to whom He wills.

James says, "Hearken, my beloved brethren, hath not God chosen the poor of this world rich in faith?" (James 2:5) One cannot hold one's riches to oneself and at the same time wield that faith that subdues kingdoms, works righteousness, stops the mouths of lions, quenches the violence of fire, resurrects the dead, etc. (Hebrews 11). One can have great knowledge of doctrines and dogmas and Bible truths, which are called "The Faith," but not have that word of faith which the Lord confirms with signs following. This is the reason that He is able to do many more miracles amongst the very poor of India or Indonesia, where riches are not a barrier, than among the members of the more affluent churches of the West.

The Example of Jesus

Let us consider the earthly life of the Lord Jesus, for He ever practiced His own precepts. How and where was the Lord born? He was born in a stable, and cradled in a manger. When Mary and Joseph came to Jerusalem to dedicate the Baby to the Lord, they offered a pair of turtle doves or two young pigeons (Luke 2:21-24). Reference to this offering in Leviticus 12:6-8 reveals that it was the offering of poverty—provision made for the poor who could not afford to bring a lamb. Where was Jesus reared? Amongst the poor and uneducated.

Did Jesus of Nazareth have an education like Paul? No! "How knoweth this Man letters [Greek: *gramma;* i.e., "the writings"], having never learned?" (John 7:15) "Can any good thing come out of Nazareth?" (John 1:46) Jesus was brought up to be a carpenter, not one who necessarily worked only in wood, but one who was an artisan, working also in iron and stone. He was of ordinary stock, one of the common, useful, humble people. If He had lived nowadays, His surname could likely have been "Smith." He belonged to none of the exclusive circles, the rich, the educated, or the aristocracy. This enabled Him to speak on faith. Faith was a great necessity to One who had neither a hole like a fox nor a nest like a bird—"not where to lay His head" (Luke 9:58). Are then Christ's true and poor disciples entirely dependent on the charity of kindly disposed people? Never! Rather, their dependence is on the ever-flowing bounty of an all-providing Heavenly Father!

An Example from Church History

Here is one of the Lord's humble poor, the Rev. John Wesley, a man of faith. See now how he follows His Master. We will take just one incident of many from his journals. He is eighty-one years old at the time of this entry:

> *1785, Tuesday, January 4th.*
>
> *At this season we usually distribute coals and bread among the poor of the society. But I now considered that they wanted clothes as well as food. So on this and the four following days I walked through the town [London] and begged two hundred pounds, in order to clothe them that needed it most. But it was hard work, as most of the streets were filled with melting snow, which often lay ankle deep; so that my feet were steeped in snow-water from morning 'till evening. I held out pretty well 'till Saturday evening; but I was laid out with a violent flux which increased every*

hour, 'till, at six in the morning, Dr. Whitehead called upon me. His first draught made me quite easy; and three or four more perfected the cure.

By contrast, to make the light shine clear against the darkness, consider one of the usual clergy of those days. Here is an extract from the diary of Parson Woodforde[2] of this period. He details one of his usual dinners:

...A fine pike roasted for dinner with a Pudding in his Belly; a leg of mutton with caper sauce, a pig's face, a neck of pork roasted with gooseberries and a plum pudding and eggs, roast fowl, orange pudding; custards and jellies.

And for supper, which in England would be just before going to bed:

...A brace of partridges, some cold tongue, potatoes in shells, meat pies and more tarts...

Can you see more clearly why the clergy of Parson Woodforde's type despised, scoffed at, and maligned John Wesley? Parson Woodforde on Sunday would read to his congregation a homily on "Justification by Faith." Yet what did he know of the scripture that "God hath chosen the poor of this world rich in faith" (James 2:5)? John Wesley, however, knew it in deed and in truth.

More Examples from Jesus' Life

See again, how the Lord's poverty brought Him to the necessity of faith. Matthew records how the collectors for the Temple authority came to obtain the half-shekel tribute which they exacted from every Jew. Jesus had no money, nor had Peter. Their poverty necessitated a miracle; it was done! Peter was commanded to angle for a fish—and how wonderful: the one he caught had a *stater* in its mouth (a coin introduced by the Romans that had the value of a shekel), and this he paid for Jesus and himself (Matthew 17:24-27).

The Lord's very first miracle was wrought out of poverty. The wedding party had no wine; the wine merchants had. But this required money; and very gladly would the merchants have delivered more wine if the money had been forthcoming. Jesus was poor, but rich in faith and compassion. His poverty necessitated a miracle. He turned water into wine (John 2:1-11).

Again there came a time when a great multitude heard Him and hung on His words as the hours slipped by. With the approach of evening, the sun had begun to set. It was a desert place. The multitude was hungry and would have to go fainting away. If Jesus had been rich, His foreknowledge would have provided ample food. There were food merchants in the cities where the people had come from who could have provisioned an army. Had He possessed worldly wealth, Jesus could have ordered the food from them for such a time and at such a place, and paid the money, and a cavalcade of camels, mules and asses would have brought it there. But Jesus was poor; and saying, "I have compassion on the multitude," out of the riches of His divine faith, the faith of the Son of God, He took five barley loaves and two fishes, and fed to the full five thousand men, besides women and children (John 6:1-13).

Are You Rich or Poor?

Whenever the church increases in political power, pride and wealth, her glory dies with her poverty. The Lord Jesus said, "Thou sayest, I am rich" (Revelation 3:17). Do not the major denominations tell us of the extent of their properties, their magnificent buildings, their earthly possessions and their mortgages? But listen again to the word of the Lord: "Thou sayest, I am rich and increased with goods, and have need of nothing, and knowest not that thou art wretched, and miserable, and poor, and blind, and naked" (Revelation 3:17). The story is told of a pope, his heart swelling with pride as he looked around on the glories of the Vatican and as he thought of the wealth represented by the curia of which he was the head. "Our founder, St. Peter," said he to a cardinal, "could say, 'Silver and gold have I none,' but we," said he smilingly, "could not say that." "No," thoughtfully replied the cardinal, "nor can we say, 'Take up thy bed and walk!' "[3]

True faith, then, cannot be exercised without poverty of spirit. It is not the fact of being poor that enables the operation of faith. Poverty alone can militate against it. The "cares of this world" can choke the seed of the Word as effectually as can its opposite, the "deceitfulness of riches" (Matthew 13:22). It is this blessed "Sister Poverty" whom Francis of Assisi knew so well, this meekness and lowliness of spirit, that takes with joy the privilege of being wholly dependent on its Beloved, which is the fruitful ground for the planting and growth of the tree of Faith. This lowly spirit has the spirit of forgiveness; the spirit of forgiveness ever walks hand in hand with the spirit of confession. "Confess your faults one to another and pray one for another that ye may be healed" (James 5:16). This does not mean that the one seeking healing should confess *his* faults; that has already been covered in verse 15. It means, let the elders of the church who have come to lay hands upon the sick one and to anoint him with oil in the name of the Lord confess *their* faults one to another, in true poverty of spirit, that the riches of faith might be released. If this were done more often, we would see more miracles of healing. More will be said concerning the conditions which enable faith to increase when we come to consider the life and growth of faith.

Endnotes for Chapter 2

1. *Smoking flax*, i.e., a dimly burning wick
2. Rev. James Woodforde (1740–1803) was an Anglican clergyman who kept a long-running diary, later published in the Twentieth Century under the title *The Diary of a Country Parson.*
3. See Acts 3:6.

·3· The Nature of Faith

New Covenant Language, Old Covenant Experience

The true weakness of the evangelical fundamentalism of today is that it exercises New Covenant speech from an Old Covenant experience. This is a recurring problem in the Church, and it is only solved for many when the Holy Spirit comes into the midst of His people in revival power, and reigns sovereignly as Lord. There is too much mechanical Christianity.

A fundamentalist in this sense is one who believes that a person is born of God, is in Christ, and is a spiritual man indwelt by the Holy Spirit because he believes in the infallibility of the Scriptures and accepts all of the fundamental truths taught therein. But the true son of God has not been made so by the Bible. The Bible cannot give life, but only point the way to life. The Lord Jesus Christ alone is the Life, and He alone can give it. He gave this life to many thousands in the early days of the Church, before ever the New Testament was written, and when the great majority of the Church, being of the poorest class, were unable to read the Scriptures of the Old Testament either in the Hebrew or the Greek.

The Pharisees worshiped the Torah, and placed it above the Messiah. They believed in all of the miracles recorded in the Scriptures, but refused to believe in even one miracle performed by the Son of God before their eyes. They were dispensationalists. They had compressed the almighty and eternal God into a number of Scriptural, reasonable, theological, hermetically-sealed, water-tight compartments. They said that signs and wonders used to happen, and that to be sound, one must believe this. Miracles, they said, do not happen anymore, but what is happening must be put down either to human imagination stimulated by emotion, or to the devil. Jesus said to them, "Search the Scriptures; for in them ye think ye have eternal life: and they are they which testify of Me. And ye will not come unto Me, that ye might have life" (John 5:39,40). The Lord was saying to them that eternal life is not in the Scriptures, which are given to reveal Him in whom alone is eternal life. These Pharisees, typical of that kind of fundamentalism of which they are the biblical figure, thought that eternal life lay in the believing, the perusing, and the learning by heart of the Scriptures. They placed Scripture above the Person to whom it was only the guide—the way to the only Way to God.

It is true that a regenerate person, a child of God, believes in the full inspiration of the Bible; but it is untrue to assume that because one accepts the inspiration of the Scriptures, and consequently its truths, therefore one must be a child of God. All of God's children are born from *above*, not from anything below, whether it be flesh or blood, the sincere will of man,[1] or even the Scriptures. They are born only through spiritual conception by the Holy Spirit. Yet people are taught by some that if they believe the truth of a certain scripture, then automatically they have the experience referred to in that scripture. This is not the faith of God; it is human believism.

Too many have abandoned the position of being subject to the law of Moses, only to be subjected to a new code of laws concocted for them from the writings of Paul by well-meaning people. They are still under the law. Their life then consists of

Scriptural legalities, and they test themselves and each other by outward conformity to certain inspired Pauline words of advice; whereas the true test of the life is the manifestation of the fruit of the Spirit—practical holiness, which is positive righteousness motivated by love. They have that withdrawing and repelling thing, legal righteousness. But "if the Son therefore shall make you free, ye shall be free indeed" (John 8:36). The Word of God says, "The letter killeth, but the Spirit giveth life" (2 Corinthians 3:6). Man's side of the Old Covenant was that he should keep the law. The law was given in great clarity, and engraved in letters upon tablets of stone. But while the Lord Jehovah was confirming the law and writing it Himself, the people were breaking it. Moses confirmed that they had already done this and had broken the covenant, when he himself smashed the engraved terms of the covenant to pieces (Exodus 32:19). This was the giving of law by letter; there is always death in the letter of the law. The Lord God of Israel then bade the sons of Levi to go through the camp and slay the breakers of the law, "and there fell of the people that day *about three thousand* men" (Exodus 32:27,28). Truly, "the letter killeth." This is the Old Covenant of law, out of which we come into the New Covenant of Grace, the law being "our schoolmaster [Greek: *paidagōgos*—"child conductor"] to bring us unto Christ" (Galatians 3:24). But what a different heralding there is to the Covenant of Grace!

There is an old Jewish tradition that Pentecost is the anniversary of the original giving of the law. If that is true, then it makes the descent of the Holy Spirit, recorded in the second chapter of Acts, even more interesting. The Holy Spirit was given by the Father, and was received by the Son so that He might shower His love-gift upon all believers as the pledge and earnest of their inheritance under the New Covenant. So He confirmed His covenant by reversing the sentence of death under the Old Covenant of law, because the "Spirit giveth life" (2 Corinthians 3:6); and "the same day there were added unto them *about three thousand* souls" (Acts 2:41). The nature of faith under the New Covenant is in the *Spirit*—not under the letter of a law. We are not brought to new birth by the acceptance of a formula—even though it be a statement of truth taken from the Bible—but by an act of the Holy Spirit who, in Almighty power, effects the new birth from above. It is a miracle.

The Realm of Faith

Faith is "the evidence of things not seen." Faith, like its Author, is transcendent; it is outside the world of physical contact. Just as one cannot see a sound, or smell a sunset, or hear the scent of a violet, or feel (by touching) the beauty of a landscape, because we are applying physical tests in the wrong realms of dimension, so faith is outside of feeling, sight, or sound. Faith, to be effectual, must also be immanent, that is, indwelling. It is evidence itself of an inner truth known by the recipient as having been given by God, and it is absolutely real. Faith may be an abstract noun, but it is a concrete thing. Faith is not of the same quality as "belief." It is not in that realm. Faith is in the realm of consciousness. To believe that one is in a certain state of being, and to be conscious of the truth of such a state, are two entirely different things. For example, a mental patient suffering from paranoia can really believe that he is, shall we say, the President of the United States, and whilst affected by this form of psychosis he will speak and act in conformity with his delusion. His very circumstances demonstrate the fact that although he is completely sincere in his belief, his belief is an error, a delusion. But what of *consciousness* of truth? This is in the realm of self-knowledge and personal experience, and although known to the one who has it, cannot be given or transferred by him to anyone else. "Hast thou faith? Have it to thyself before God" (Romans 14:22). A person can no more be reasoned into faith than he can be reasoned into the witness of the Spirit. Yet it is a primary

Christian duty to pass on the good news that this gift of God will be given by Him to every sincere, seeking soul who will come to Him as a little child. For Jesus said, "Whosoever shall not receive the kingdom of God as a little child shall in no wise enter therein" (Luke 18:17).

Believers in God, being in the new birth, have the nature of little children, and if they will continue in that life, they will mature, as the apostle John makes clear, from being "little children" to becoming "young men" and from "young men" to "fathers" (1 John 2:12-14). The Holy Spirit, in Luke 18, has pointed out the steps to this childlike faith into the Kingdom:

- An importunate widow desires something and, just like a little child, she asks for it until she gets it (verses 1-5). This is the childlike way of asking.
- A publican goes to the Temple and calls upon God to forgive the sinner. He offers to God no reason why He should do so, because he knows that there are no reasons to give. He was just feeling that he was the worst man in the world (verses 9-14). This is the childlike way of confessing.
- A sophisticated young ruler cannot follow the childlike way of faith (verses 18-23), which is to drop whatever glittering thing one has in hand for the more wonderful thing offered by the Father; but this is the childlike way of accepting.
- The disciples had left all and were following Him (verses 28-30), but now He was saying things that greatly puzzled them; for although they still believed in Him, they did not understand. Yet they continued with Him just the same. This is the childlike way of following.

- At the end of this 18th chapter of Luke there is the account of a blind beggar who received his sight (verses 35-43). So glad was he, that without any embarrassment, before all the people, he followed Jesus, glorifying God. This is the childlike way of testifying.

Faith has no difficulties for the childlike heart, because faith's very nature is simplicity.

God's Revelation of Faith in the Story of Naaman

We must now look at God's revelation of faith. He has clearly defined the nature of faith and the nature of its opposite, unbelief, in the sublimely inspired story of Naaman. It would be to your advantage to compare the following teaching with the Scriptures. Refer to 2 Kings 5.

Representatives of Unbelief

Let us deal first with unbelief. Faith and unbelief are diametrically opposite and mutually antagonistic. Faith is belief of the revealed truth; unbelief is refusal to believe. It is not ignorance of the truth, which is non-belief. The Most High will deal with the ignorant far differently from those who have seen the truth, but have refused to walk in it. To rightly understand the nature of faith, we must look first at the qualities of unbelief. These are represented in the story of Naaman by Naaman's wife, the King of Syria, the King of Israel, and Gehazi. By considering these we may understand the basic foundations of unbelief.

Naaman's Wife: Selfishness

Like the wife of Noah and the wife of Lot, the name of Naaman's wife is not mentioned in Scripture. The reason usually advanced to explain this is the relative unimportance of the woman as compared with the man in Bible days. There is a faint gleam of truth in this, but in view of the large number of women and wives who *are* named, the gleam is very faint indeed. Jehovah is the God of Abraham, Isaac and Jacob and none the less of their wives, who are all named. The real reason that the wife of Naaman is not named may well be in the Scriptures: "The name of the wicked shall rot" (Proverbs 10:7), while "the righteous shall be in everlasting remembrance" (Psalm 112:6). **She reveals in her nature a potent cause of unbelief—selfishness**, that is, an uncrucified self. Naaman's wife receives all and gives nothing. Pampered, luxurious, waited upon by slaves, she has no compassion. She is cold, indifferent, and self-centered. She would lament the fact that she had the misfortune to be married to a man who had contracted leprosy, but not that her afflicted husband had this dreadful disease. Notice that the little maid (2 Kings 5:3) told her mistress of the great prophet of Israel who could cure leprosy. One would have thought that she would have flown to give Naaman the good news. Not she! "One went in, and told his lord..." (2 Kings 5:4). It was carried to him secondhand by one who overheard the conversation. Selfishness is frigid, compassionless, and unbelieving. Selfishness hears of mighty works and miracles and of One who has compassion, but is dead to it all, like "the deaf adder that stoppeth her ear; which will not hearken to the voice of charmers, charming never so wisely" (Psalm 58:4,5).

King of Syria: Superstition

The second ground of unbelief is *superstition*. Wise John Bunyan, over three hundred years ago, in *Pilgrim's Prog-*

ress, revealed how superstition opposes faith. Christian and Faithful have been arrested and are being tried for their lives in the town of Vanity Fair. Lord Hate-good is the judge, and among the witnesses against Faithful is old Superstition. Listen carefully to Superstition's testimony and take note of Faithful's inspired reply:

> ***Superstition:*** *"My lord, I have no great acquaintance with this man, nor do I desire to have further knowledge of him... however, the other day... I heard him say that our religion was naught, and such by which a man could by no means please God... [it] follows that we do worship in vain and are yet in our sins and finally shall be damned."*

> ***Faithful:*** *"I said only this, that in the worship of God there is required a divine faith; but there can be no divine faith without a divine revelation of the will of God. Therefore, whatever is thrust into the worship of God that is not agreeable to divine revelation cannot be done but by a human faith, which faith will not be profitable to eternal life."*

Superstition is maintained by credulity, not faith. Credulity is a disposition to believe without satisfactory evidence; it arrives at its conclusions through impulse and emotion and by the influence of heredity. That is why there are often better grounds for faith outside of the organized churches than within. An evangelist can take the message of Divine healing to a well-established church and find little response; he takes the same message to the "heathen," and thousands are saved and healed.

The King of Syria knows nothing of the individual walk with God; he thinks that the religion of the country is always identifiable with the government of the state. Therefore, he writes to his counterpart and rival, the King of Israel, about healing for his commander-in-chief, Naaman. "Now when this letter is come unto thee, behold, I have therewith sent Naaman my servant to thee, that thou mayest recover him of his leprosy" (2 Kings 5:6). The idea was that the King of Israel would order his servant-prophet Elisha to do the cure, and Elisha would bow himself to the ground and say, "It shall be done my lord, O King; may you live forever" (although he knew that he wouldn't), and go and do it. The King of Israel would then give him a small portion of "the ten talents of silver and six thousand pieces of gold," whilst he himself kept the major portion and the "ten changes of raiment." By analogy, the King is the wholesaler, Elisha the retailer, and Naaman the customer. It all sounds very modern.

The King of Syria held the doctrine of what has become known as *Erastianism*, that the State has supreme authority over the church. This doctrine was once held in England, when the people were controlled by the crown through the Church of England; in Russia, when the serfs were enslaved through the government-controlled Russian Orthodox Church; and in Prussia, under the State Lutheran Church. This is the great significance of the First Amendment to the Constitution of the United States of America (adopted December 15, 1791) which reads: "Congress shall make no law respecting an establishment of religion, or prohibiting the free exercise thereof...." It was made to prevent the practice of Erastianism in any one of the States of the Union and not, emphatically *not*, to prohibit the Bible or Christianity from its schools, colleges, and universities. One would have thought that the Supreme Court would have seen a simple thing like that.

The King of Israel: Fear

The third ground of unbelief is *fear*. Fear is one of Satan's master weapons. Just as the Kingdom of Heaven is established upon faith, hope and love, so is the kingdom of hell founded upon their opposites, unbelief, fear and hate. The Lord

Jesus says that at the end of the age the "distress of nations, with perplexity" shall lead to "men's hearts failing them for fear" (Luke 21:25,26). He says, "When the Son of Man cometh, shall He find faith on the earth?" (Luke 18:8) The god of this world, through the *zeitgeist*—the spirit of the age—has everything controlled to cause fear. Films, newspapers, fiction, television, the stage, are all aimed to scare the mind and make the flesh creep. Even some Christian radio stations add their portion by teaching the people the seditious idea, the disloyal untruth, that the Bible says that soon all America must go under Communism.[2] The Bible says not a word about it. The devil will do anything to panic the sheep and get them on the run. Even horror comics are provided for the children. To complete the circle, we have fear of environmental pollution, fear of the population explosion, and fear of the atomic bomb. But not for you, believing Christian, for:

The hosts of God encamp around
The dwellings of the just,
Deliv'rance He affords to all
Who on His succour trust.

* * *

Fear Him, ye saints, and you will then
Have nothing else to fear;
Make you His service your delight,
He'll make your wants His care."[3]

—Tate and Brady, 17th Century—

Poor King of Israel, bound by fear! "He rent his clothes" and did what governments, influenced by fear, always do: misinterpret the intention of the rulers of the other nation—a potent trigger of war. "Consider, I pray you, and see how he seeketh a quarrel against me" (2 Kings 5:7). And he didn't know that there was a prophet, a man of God, who had God-given faith to heal leprosy, who lived in his very kingdom.

All these people are blind and deaf. Naaman's wife cannot see the answer to her husband's need; she cannot hear the little maid. The King of Syria cannot see that it is to the man of God that Naaman should go, and that the King of Israel has nothing to do with it. He does not know that, as Peter warned Simon Magus, the gift of God cannot be purchased with money (Acts 8:20). The King of Israel cannot see that there is a prophet in Israel. Unbelief is blind and deaf, selfish and without compassion, and superstitiously religious.

Gehazi: Faithlessness

But what shall we say of Gehazi? How blind and deaf to light and truth he is! He is always in the company of the man of God, but he does not see, hear, or know God. There are many who live in the household of God's prophets, who are blind; children of godly parents can go astray. So obtuse to the grace of God is Gehazi, ***so faithless***, that he uses the miracles of God to obtain wealth. Are there not today some preachers who do the same, using the miracles of God to obtain money, their ambition being to have a renowned name, wealth and praise? "Is it," said Elisha to Gehazi, "a time to receive money, and to receive garments [to wear expensive clothes], and olive yards and vineyards [to get estates], and sheep and oxen [to acquire ranches], and menservants, and maidservants [a great personal establishment with a palatial central office]?" (2 Kings 5:26) Well, *is* it? Gehazi got what Naaman was willing to give up—wealth; but he also got what always goes with the world's wealth—the world's leprosy. That is why he got Naaman's leprosy.

Representatives of Faith

What a relief to turn from this darkness and death to light and life; for in this story we also have the record of faith. The Holy Spirit clearly gives us here living examples of the qualities that make up the nature of faith: the servant who went in and told his lord, the little maid, Elisha, the servants of Naaman, and Naaman himself. It will be most profitable to think about these.

The One Who Told His Lord: The Record of Faith

This is the average Christian. His testimony to God's great miracle power and supernatural manifestations is secondhand. It is what he has read or heard about, but he believes it and he passes the information on. It helps; it is a link in the chain. **This is the *record* of faith.**

The Little Maid: The Basis of Faith

Here with a few deft touches the Holy Spirit sketches for us one of the most loving, most gracious, most Jesus-like characters revealed in the Bible. Who was she? Of what tribe and family did she come? What was her name? No one but God knows anything of her earthly parentage, except that she was of the land of Israel. Why is her name not revealed? For an excellent reason: she shares with Rebekah and Ruth the honor of being one of the types of the Bride, the Lamb's wife. Why is the name of the Bride not given in Scripture? It is because the bride has the privilege of taking her husband's name. The little maid, like the Church, is a servant. In this she follows her Lord, who is celebrated in the "Servant Songs" of Isaiah[4] as the perfect Servant of Jehovah. The little maid, like the Church, is a stranger in a strange land; this world is not the Church's home. The Church is a witnessing Church, like the little maid, and a Church whose spirit is love, like the spirit of the little maid.

The little maid reveals the *basis* of faith, which is *love*. From this ground, this base, this solid foundation of love, proceed all the works of faith—"Faith which worketh by love" (Galatians 5:6). Why did the Lord Jesus do His mighty works of healing the sick, delivering the bound (that is, the demon-possessed), and raising the dead? He did them from one motive only: "He was moved with compassion" (Matthew 9:36). He did not do His deeds of power to manifest His glory, as some say. This is not the nature of Him who is meek and lowly in heart. He healed because He loved the people. What confidence has the little maid! "Would God my lord were with the prophet that is in Samaria! for he would recover him of his leprosy" (2 Kings 5:3). *Confidence is the essence of faith.* Each one of these representatives of faith in the story of Naaman has this in common. She says, "He would recover him." Elisha says, "Let him come now to me" (2 Kings 5:8). The servants of Naaman say, "How much rather then, when he saith to thee, 'Wash and be clean?' " (2 Kings 5:13) Naaman does not doubt his healing, but prefers the clear waters of Abana and Pharpar to the rather discolored waters of the Jordan. They are all sure that it is going to happen. Hold on to confidence. If you have prayed and you know that your prayer is in the will of God, and the answer is long delayed, then the situation calls for confidence, not collapse. Confidence is the strengthening, steadying warp and woof of the texture of faith. Here is a true verse on this:

He says He'll carry all my care,
If by His side I'll stay;
He also bids me not to cast
My confidence away.
But oh! how foolishly I act,
When taken unaware;

I cast away my confidence
And carry all my care.[5]

—James Seward—

Now consider the virtue of this little maid. Why was her witness accepted? Because of her credibility; her life was consistent with her words. The primary purpose of the gift of the Holy Spirit is that we should be witnesses unto the Lord Jesus. This does not mean that we have been given a gift of volubility. Communists, Mormons, and Jehovah's Witnesses all have this in common. It is not because of the Holy Spirit that they gush in persuasive talk, but because—I borrow an Irish phrase—"They have kissed the blarney stone," or, as a cockney Londoner would say, "They've got the gift of the gab." What the Holy Spirit does when He comes in is to make our witness credible; that is, what we are and what we say are identical—we manifest Jesus and we talk about Jesus from the Spirit of Jesus, who is in and upon us. What the captivity of this little maid meant to the healing of Naaman can be seen from the following considerations.

Naaman would not have been healed unless the little maid had been a captive, far away from where she longed to be. This was her cross; but she took it up and bore it, and shone just where she was. Naaman would not have been healed if she had not had a broken heart. She often thought of her father and mother, her home, her brothers and sisters, and her own lovely country. Consider this, for the Lord is willing to teach you that all the long years of your frustrations, your troubles, and your heartaches are for a purpose—to forge a strong and mighty faith in you. There are those, hidden from public view, who are to be used of God in the coming revival. They only dimly see, if they see at all, His purpose in all of their hindrances and losses; but they are like John the Baptist, who "was in the deserts till the day of his showing unto Israel" (Luke 1:80). How like the Lord is the little maid. What heartaches, what suffering, what groanings in spirit were the lot of Jesus, far from His home where dwelt His Father.

Who caused the pains and tears of the little maid? The very one whom she sought to deliver—Naaman, the chief of all those marauding bands who had destroyed her pleasant home, murdered her family and friends, and preserved her only to make her a slave. Who caused Jesus' pains and tears? The very ones whom He came to deliver. How freely did the little maid forgive Naaman! She might have found means to murder him, if she had been inclined. She could easily have dropped some oleander cuttings into his soup. Her name would then have become known and renowned in Jewish national history, and have been linked with Jael, who slew Sisera (Judges 4:17-24), or with Judith, who murdered Holofernes.[6] But she had the spirit of love, the Spirit of Jesus: "While we were yet sinners, Christ died for us" (Romans 5:8). She had been free, but she became a slave, in order that the one who had enslaved her might be made free from the tyranny of leprosy. So Jesus "took upon Him the form of a servant... He humbled Himself, and became obedient" (Philippians 2:7-8), because "when we were enemies, we were reconciled to God by the death of His Son" (Romans 5:10). Love is the basis of faith.

Elisha, the Man of God: The Character of Faith

Elisha reveals the *character* of faith, that is, the character of a man or a woman of faith. No book learning can give you faith; reading this book will not give it to you. There is no method to be learned to obtain faith. It is only by "abiding in Him" that "we ask what we will" and it is done for us (John 15:7). ***The man or woman of God has three essential enduements:***

1. ***The first enduement is authority*** (Greek: *exousia*). This is the possession of every true son of God. John says, "As many as received Him, to them gave He power [authority] to become the sons of God, even to them that believe on His name: Which were born, not of blood, nor of the will of the flesh, nor of the will of man, but of God" (John 1:12). This authority is given only to those able to carry it by reason of the indwelling of the Most High God. As the Christian's spiritual stature increases, authority is manifested in ever-increasing measure; hence the exercise of ever-increasing faith.

2. ***The second enduement from God*** to form the character of the man of faith ***is power*** (Greek: *dunamis*). It is recorded in the Acts of the Apostles that the disciples received power after the Holy Spirit had come upon them at Pentecost, according to the promise of the Lord (Acts 1:8; Acts 2:1-4). But authority takes precedence over power, for it is the God-given, legitimate ability to exercise command, and is part of the nature of the person wielding it. Yet, whereas *authority* must always proceed from and be a part of the nature of the one exercising it, *power*, as manifested in a supernatural act, is a gift given by God to the person using it. Solomon was a man with great God-given authority, as his majesty reveals; but there is no record of his ever having performed any miracles (although there are non-biblical legends enough about him and his magical doings). Samson, on the other hand, did his miracles of acts of strength by the power of God given to him under the anointing of the Spirit; but he seems sadly lacking in the commanding majesty of inspired authority. The man of God has both.

3. ***The third enduement from God is holiness***. The man of God abides in Christ; he keeps His commandments;

his heart has been purified by faith. His is not a mythical Christ, nor a Bible Christ, nor a historical Christ, nor even One in the heavens who may be occasionally brought down and received through bread and wine in the sacrament. His is the indwelling Christ. The Living Word is nigh him, in his heart. Christ is in him, the hope of glory; and as he dwells in the sinless, incorruptible new birth, and as by a living faith he abides in this inner Christ, he sins not. Then is fulfilled in him the words of Peter, "If any man speak, let him speak as the oracles of God" (1 Peter 4:11). But what an astonishing word to some this is, for the oracles of God are the Scriptures. Unto the Jews, says Paul (Roman 3:2), "were committed the oracles of God." So the man of God speaks in faith, from the same Spirit which gave forth the Scriptures. His words have substance; he speaks and it is done. The evidence is there, for God lets "none of His words fall to the ground" (1 Samuel 3:19). His word is confirmed with signs following. This is no vain borrowing from the Scriptures, no guesswork, no uttering of a scriptural lesson, no repetition of a text committed to memory; no, he speaks the very word of God. "Go," says Elisha, "and wash in Jordan seven times, and thy flesh shall come again to thee, and thou shalt be clean... And his flesh came again like unto the flesh of a little child, and he was clean" (2 Kings 5:10,14).

The Servants of Naaman: The Mind of Faith

Naaman's servants represent the *mind* of faith—the humble mind. There was a great barrier standing in the way of Naaman's healing: his pride. Humility is not always the accompanying mark of the evangelist of healing, but it ought to be, for divine faith and human pride are of opposite natures; like oil and water, they will not mix. God stands aloof from the proud, but He is nigh to the humble heart.

Blest are the humble souls that see
Their emptiness and poverty;
Treasures of grace to them are given,
And crowns of joy laid up in heaven.[7]

—Isaac Watts—

"My father," said the servants (who, in their humble sphere of submission, had learned wisdom), "if the prophet had bid thee do some great thing, wouldest thou not have done it? How much rather then, when he saith to thee, 'Wash and be clean?' " (2 Kings 5:13). Faith is attendant upon a humble mind. This is the mind of Christ. Every newborn saint, that is, every child of God, already has this mind. It is not a thing to be zealous for, or to reach out after, or to discipline oneself to obtain. "We have the mind of Christ" (1 Corinthians 2:16); it is a part of the new birth, to be exercised. Peter says, "I stir up your pure minds" (2 Peter 3:1). This is why humility and faith for healing go together. Consider the Scriptures: "If My people... shall *humble* themselves... then will I... heal" (2 Chronicles 7:14). Again, "When they were sick... I *humbled* my soul with fasting" (Psalm 35:13).

This is the great reason why mighty miracles are usually performed through the agency of little things, very contemptible little things, too, in the eyes of the world; for even the very wise still look for God's kings in palaces rather than in stables. God used a bush, perhaps a scrub tamarisk, to manifest His glory and arrest the attention of Moses. Moses demonstrated the almighty power of Jehovah through the simple use of a dry stick—his rod. Samson's strength lay not in the size of his body, nor the development of his muscles, for the Philistines were completely at a loss to discover where his great strength lay.

Samson, full of the Spirit, picked up the new jawbone of a dead ass and slew heaps upon heaps of the enemies of the Lord. The Living God still uses the same principle, but in reverse: many have entered into life when He has deigned to use as an instrument the "new jawbone of an ass." Think, too, of the widow's "handful of meal" and "a little oil in a cruse" (1 Kings 17:12), and the miracles of Jesus done with such common and usual things as water, barley bread, a fish, or mud made with spittle; it is all one, with the Lord having "chosen the poor of this world rich in faith" (James 2:5).

Naaman reveals the *practice* of faith; but that is such an important subject that it must share with faith's problems a chapter of its own.

The thing surpasses all my thought,
But faithful is my Lord;
Through unbelief I stagger not,
For God hath spoke the word.

Faith, mighty faith, the promise sees,
And looks to that alone,
Laughs at impossibilities,
And cries, "It shall be done!"[8]

—Charles Wesley—

ENDNOTES FOR CHAPTER 3

1. An allusion to John 1:13
2. The first edition of this book was published in 1975, when the Cold War was still very much in the minds of people on both sides of the Iron Curtain.
3. From the hymn ***Through All the Changing Scenes of Life***, found in

---

the appendix on page 182.

4. The "Servant Songs" are certain of the Messianic passages in the Book of Isaiah, chiefly 42:1-9; 49:1-13; 50:4-11; and 52:13—53:12.

5. From the poem *His Will*

6. Pastor Gutteridge refers to a story in the Apocrypha, found in the Book of Judith.

7. From Watts's hymn ***Blest Are the Humble Souls That See***, a restatement of the Beatitudes in verse. See the entire hymn on page 184.

8. See Wesley's entire hymn, ***Father of Jesus Christ, My Lord*** in the appendix, page 185.

·4·
The Practice and Problems of Faith

Living by Faith

FAITH MUST BE ACTIVE, that is, a *working* faith, else it is not true faith. James says concerning Abraham, "Seest thou how faith wrought with his works, and by works was faith made perfect?" (James 2:22) The inspired word is clear, plain, and unalterable: "Faith without works is dead" (James 2:20); that is, without works, true faith is non-existent. This does not mean that the child of God is always working miracles. It means that the conduct of his life demonstrates that he lives by faith. William Tyndale, forever renowned as the one who, overcoming all opposition, translated the New Testament and had it distributed in England, and who was martyred for his faith (being strangled and burned at Vilvorde near Antwerp in 1536), thus explains faith:

> *The believing of God's promises, and a sure trust in the goodness and truth of God; which faith justified Abraham (Genesis 15), and was the mother of all his good works which he afterwards did. For faith is the goodness of all works in the sight of God. Good works are things of God's commandment wrought in faith. And to sew a shoe at the commandment of God, to do thy neighbour service withal, with faith to be saved by Christ (as God promiseth us), is much better than to build an abbey of thine own imagina-*

> *tion, trusting to be saved by the feigned works of hypocrites.*[1]

There is a loose expression concerning certain persons who are not in wage-earning employment, or who are not receiving a regular salary as ministers of a denominational church, that they are "living by faith." Let it be clearly said and always maintained that it is not a mark of extra spirituality that one is not in receipt of a salary. Many a salaried minister will hear the Lord's glad welcoming word, "Well done, good and faithful servant" (Matthew 25:21). Nevertheless, the Lord has called some to trust Him alone for support, because the nature of their calling does not permit them to locate. It will be found that the Lord's provision will work out, on an average, to be neither less nor more than that of those whom He has appointed to serve a local church or parish.

Active Faith

So faith must be active; the man of faith must do something. But what must he do? Only that which the Lord has told him to do, in a direct word from Him. Usually that word will come from the Scriptures, because the "word of the Lord endureth for ever" (1 Peter 1:25), and what God has once said is true for all eternity. But the Lord may choose to say something that He has not said before or that has not been recorded in writing, or in the Scriptures; for out of His mouth *still* goes a sharp two-edged sword. On at least two occasions He spoke to two of His children through a verse from the Apocrypha.[2] John Bunyan, author of *Pilgrim's Progress*, says:

> *One day... as I was giving up the ghost of all my hopes of ever attaining life, that sentence fell with weight upon my spirit, "Look at the generation of old and see; did any ever trust in the Lord and was confounded?" At which I was*

> *greatly encouraged in my soul... So coming home, I presently went to my Bible... for it was with such strength and comfort on my spirit that it was as if it talked with me. Well I looked but I found it not... thus I continued above a year, and could not find the place; but at last casting my eye upon the Apocrypha books, I found it in Ecclesiasticus 2:10*[3] *... that word doth still oftimes shine before my face.*[4]

In the second instance, on October 30, 1738, George Whitefield was on a homeward journey to England from Georgia. He had left Charleston on September 9, sailing in the "Mary," and because of storms and contrary winds the passengers and crew were reduced to a daily allowance of a pint of muddy water, an ounce or two of salt beef, and some dumplings made from weevil-filled flour and "the Skimmings of the pot." Still far from home, they had a further week's voyaging to do before they came to Ireland. He says,

> *Reading... in the book of Maccabees*[5] *and thinking of my present situation, this verse was pressed with unspeakable comfort upon my soul. "After this, they went home and sung a song of thanksgiving, and praised the Lord in Heaven; because it is good, because His mercy endureth forever!"*[6]

So let the Lord speak how and by what means He will. Of one thing you may be certain, that when He speaks, the sheep will recognize the voice of the Shepherd.[7] When an act of faith is required by the Lord, He will give a commanding word leading to action; but remember that all His commands are His enablings. "Thou shalt" not only means that you *must* do it; it also means that He will make you *able* to do it. See then, Naaman must do something, as a proof and requirement of faith, but only that which the Lord tells him to do. "Go and wash in Jordan seven times" (2 Kings 5:10). The Word is quite clear, and no jot or tittle must be added or omitted. It is not just "wash"! The place—Jordan, and the manner of it—seven times, are indicated, and nothing less than complete obedience to the will of the Lord will bring His healing.

Asking "Only Once" vs. Importunity and Inward Witness

There is a teaching that the one seeking help from the Lord must ask once only, then claim the answer by faith, and believing, never ask again. What a problem of faith this has caused to many sincere people! We can only say that both Scripture and Christian experience are against it. Jesus tells us in two parables that it is not so. The importunate widow (Luke 18:1-8) asks the judge many times for help, and Jesus "spake this parable unto them to this end, that men ought always to pray, and not to faint" (Luke 18:1). He concludes with "Shall not God avenge His own elect, which cry day and night unto Him?" (Luke 18:7). Lest you should think, as some brethren might, that this is because God is demonstrating the inferiority of womanhood, by making her ask many times (an action that she is quite capable, however, of performing), Jesus gives a parallel parable about a man (Luke 11:5-8). A traveler has come in the depth of night, but the host has no bread. Going at midnight to his friend to borrow three loaves, he is requested—quite emphatically—to go away. But he keeps on asking, and because of his ***barefacedness*** (original word), he eventually gets what he came for (Luke 11:5). What should we do when we ask, but seem to get no answer from the Lord? Go on asking! Go on asking *until there comes to you the sweet inward witness that your prayer is heard! Then* ask no more, but turn your prayer to praise; for the answer is on the way and you will prove that "He is faithful that promised" (Hebrews 10:23).

Acts of Faith

It is always a principle with God that action is required for the fulfillment of faith. God asks us to do a little thing so that He can do a great one. We have to do a foolish thing, that He may do a wise one. We move a grain; He moves a mountain. We give Him two mites, and He gives us everlasting treasure in Heaven. God said,

- "Noah, build an ark! I will send a deluge." (Genesis 6:13-14)
- "Moses, stretch out your rod! I will divide the sea!" (Exodus 14:16)
- "Naaman, dip seven times! I will heal your leprosy." (2 Kings 5:10)
- "Take ye away the stone!" (said Jesus); and then, "Lazarus, come forth!" (John 11:39-44)

That is faith! Your tiny believing—your little act; then comes God's great one. In the space of a second, you believe in Jesus, and He gives you eternal life. It is not your faith that does the mighty miracle; it is the action of Almighty God. But your faith is the hinge upon which He can open His great door of miraculous opportunity. "It is too easy," said the miner's deputy to the minister who had told him that God's salvation is by faith. "But the hoist is so easy," replied the preacher. "See how easy it is to drop you a mile down into the heart of the earth and to lift twenty tons of coal to the surface." "Ah! But you are forgetting," said the miner, "the labor and cost of sinking the shaft." "And so are you!" was the reply. "What planning! What labor! What wounds and death! What cost to God! What coming down to earth in order to take you up to Heaven!"

Consider the following acts of faith and God's responses:

- Abraham is promised a country, but he has to go out to get it. "And he went out not knowing whither he went" (Hebrews 11:8). Humanly speaking, Abraham might have died halfway to Canaan, but that was not his concern; he was called to go. *He believed God and went; and because it was the Word of the Lord, it came to pass*—"And they went forth to go into the land of Canaan; and into the land of Canaan they came" (Genesis 12:5).
- A widow is promised a supply of oil, but she must start pouring out (2 Kings 4:1-7).
- Another is promised freedom from starvation, but she has to make a cake first (1 Kings 17:8-16).
- David is assured of victory over the giant, but he has to collect and sling the stone (1 Samuel 17, especially verses 40,49).

Step out on the promise of God!

Have you been told what to do? Then go and *do* it! And should you not know what to do, then wait on the Lord until He gives you the word, "for they shall not be ashamed that wait for Me" (Isaiah 49:23). You must learn to maintain your foothold upon the ground of faith—"having done all, to stand. Stand therefore!" (Ephesians 6:13). It is "the good fight of faith" (1 Timothy 6:12); you are sure to be resisted and you are sure to win through. Hold on! Wrestle! The enemy will hurl against you ten thousand burning doubts, but keep up "the shield of faith, wherewith ye shall be able to quench all the fiery darts of the wicked [one]" (Ephesians 6:16).

To be embattled with doubts is normal Christian experience, especially at the beginning of the walk of faith. But there is a vast difference between doubts hurled from the outside, and a doubting heart on the inside. If that is your trouble, ask and receive cleansing from an evil heart of unbelief (Hebrews 3:12), else you will be kept in bondage and made to grind, like Samson, in the prison house (Judges 16:21).

What About Symptoms?

A great problem to many is the advice that they have received from well-meaning people to refuse the existence of symptoms after they have been anointed for healing. There have been many tragedies through this. We all have known of persons who have received medical advice that an operation for their condition would effect a cure, but they refused surgery because they were afraid that it would be doubting God's healing power. Their symptoms continued. They were told to ignore them as if non-existent; and death followed. When will the Church learn wisdom? Truly, very often, "the children of this world are in their generation wiser than the children of light" (Luke 16:8). If symptoms of disease are there, it is untruthful to deny their existence; and the Lord will not bless untruth. If the Holy Spirit witnesses by His Word and by His infallible inward assurance that the healing has taken place, then, most certainly, deny the symptoms, because they will only proceed from the imagination, stimulated by the evil one to cause unbelief. Christian Science denies the existence of evil, disease and pain, and it teaches its deceived followers to deny the symptoms. But we deal in reality, not in imagination. Our God really heals and delivers. With a genuine healing comes the evidences that will satisfy the honest medical practitioner.

Walk in Your Own Measure of Light and Faith

You must walk in the light and faith that God gives to you. Your name is neither A. B. Simpson[8] nor Charles S. Price.[9] Those men of God were given by Him a faith to match their call, to help pioneer the message of faith at this end of the age. But do not be discouraged; you also, in your measure, shall work the works of Him who has sent you.[10] So, do not try to copy; already you have discovered that what worked for them has not worked for you. You have blamed yourself for lack of faith, but all your efforts have not increased it, because the Lord does not intend that you should walk in their shoes, but in those He provides for you alone. Walk in truth, in the light, with Him, and do not allow those siren voices which would persuade you to operate in human faith to influence you; because, before this age is ended, there will be deeds of faith done which will fulfill all that the Lord promised when He said, "Verily, verily, I say unto you, He that believeth on Me, the works that I do shall he do also; and greater works than these shall he do, because I go unto My Father" (John 14:12). For remember again and again that "they shall not be ashamed that wait for Me" (Isaiah 49:23). Wise old Matthew Henry says, "The mower loses no time when he is whetting his scythe."[11]

Faith never insists that the Most High God must work by a method of its own choosing, or even one that we would think will bring Him more glory. The glory of God is beyond the reach of man; man can neither add nor take away from it the weight of a molecule. God preserves His own glory. This should be borne in mind when we bring our petitions to God. Are you asking for the immediate conversion of your son? It might be to the glory of God and your son's establishing, in the love of the Father, that first he should go for a time into the far country.[12] Are you asking Him to correct your eyesight? It may be that it is His will that you wear spectacles. True faith does not dictate to God; it trusts Him that all is well. But you heard of some who deliberately smashed their glasses in faith, and afterward had perfect sight. True, but that is between them and their Father; it is not for you to copy. They must walk in their vision of God's light, but it is your privilege to walk on your own with God and to know and do His will. Most of those who smash their glasses or leave off their hearing aids, after having been to a great emotion-stirring meeting, take them up again. Be patient, and you will know the will of God. Also, if you have faith that you will be healed by a surgical operation, then abide in it; but you will find that that faith will not bring results if you try to apply it for healing without an operation. Again I say, keep in your measure. The word of Paul concerning prophecy also applies to healing—"whether prophecy, let us prophesy according to the proportion of faith" (Romans 12:6).

A friend of mine in England, The Rev. C. L. Parker, M.A., after he had received the Holy Spirit, was led to hold evangelistic meetings in many parts of the country, where he taught the truth that Jesus, today, still heals the sick. He told me that on one occasion he had been enthusiastically proclaiming that Jesus in Bible days had healed all that were sick, and that today there was nothing that He could not and would not do. Then he made his appeal that needy folk should come to the front, and he would pray for them and they would be healed. To his consternation, the first man who came out was an old seaman with a wooden leg. Mr. Parker suddenly learned a great truth, that there are measures of faith, and that faith for healing is different from faith for a miracle. Healing can be a process, but a miracle must be instantaneous. He called himself a thousand fools for preaching so strong a message, for he discovered that he just did not have the faith that the Lord Jesus would replace a wooden leg with a sound one; and the man was the first one in the line! With great inward trepidation he approached the believing old sailor and said, "Brother, what do you want the Lord to do for you?" Imagine his relief when the mariner replied, "It's me chest, guv'nor."

Faith and Healing

Divine or Psychic?

It has been said that all healing is divine healing. That is not true; there are psychic healing and demonic healing, too. Dr. Kurt Koch's *Between Christ and Satan* will convince any unprejudiced person that demons heal the body in order to control the mind. C. S. Lewis has pointed out in *The Screwtape Letters* that there are two major errors into which the human race can fall. One is to refuse to believe in the existence of demons, and the other is to take a vivid and unhealthy interest in them. The latter error, especially, is one of very great danger. Too many small groups, under the impression that they are progressing in the things of the Spirit, are having demon-searching sessions, to their great spiritual loss and the advancement of the kingdom of evil.

We must look more deeply into the practical differences between what is known as faith healing, and true divine healing; that is, between psychic healing (which is through the power of the mind), and the healing that is the direct action of God. Of course, the Lord can use any means or methods that He likes. But in true divine healing, the original motivating force is from Him, whilst in psychosomatic healing—with which we will include healing by means of hypnosis—the operating power is centered in the human. In the case of healing through a spiritualistic medium, it comes either from demon power or through the exercise of psychic force. All subjection of the mind, with the consequent disenthronement of the will, to any external power save that of submission to the Creator, is dangerous. The great barrier that God has erected in every human being against domination by other intelligences is the barrier of the will. No demon possession can take place whilst the will is in its God-given place—ruling on the throne of the mind. That is why we are safe in yielding our wills to God, and He never supplants the will, but rules through it, making us "both to will and to do of His good pleasure" (Philippians 2:13).

The whole pressure and seduction of temptation is to weaken the resistance of the will, so that the will of the evil one may be done through us in an act of rebellion against the will of the Holy One, which is sin. In the case of a person coming under the influence of a wrong spirit, such as a spirit of confusion or (what is so prevalent) a religious spirit, or (in the extreme case) of demon possession, there has been an actual point in time when the authority of the will was suspended and influence or entrance was made possible. Before this, there must be a softening up process. Then at some contrived point, like a sudden accident—when for a moment the action of the will was suspended—the spirit or demon was able to enter in and take partial or full control.

The ground too often is prepared by the encouragement of indiscipline. Parents who let their children do exactly what they like—sparing the rod and spoiling the child—are being very unkind. They are preparing the child's mind, with its untrained weak will, for eventual demon possession. The Bible is quite clear on this subject of training children. "Chasten thy son while there is hope, and let not thy soul spare for his crying" (Proverbs 19:18). Moses said, "Thou shalt also consider in thine heart, that, as a man chasteneth his son, so the LORD thy God chasteneth thee" (Deuteronomy 8:5). God is not asking you to be unduly severe to your son or daughter, but to discipline *yourself* to discipline your children. You are hurting them by your refusal to train them so that they may have firm and righteous wills, and so be eligible to become men and women of faith. The reason that you do not use chastisement is because, in the first place, it requires an effort and you are indolent by nature; and, in the second, it hurts your feelings to do so and you are also self-indulgent. Of course you spoil everything when you overlook many flagrant acts of disobedience, and then thrash the child only because you happen to be in a bad temper.

Walk in the Light

Now, are you afraid of demons and demon possession? You need not be. Have you noticed that neither Jesus nor any of the apostles give any instructions on how to recognize demons or to cast out demons from His children? The apostles would be greatly surprised and amazed if they could read the syllabus of a modern Bible College course with its subject of "Demonology"—very flattering to and free advertisement for demons. The reason that we are given no such instructions is, of course, that we are children of the light, not of darkness; demons will not come into the light, because their deeds are evil. Heaven, the abode of light, would be a worse hell to a demon than Hell is. Go on walking in the light; you will then have fellowship with God, while all the time the blood of the Lord Jesus Christ is cleansing you from all sin, for "what communion hath light with darkness? And what concord hath Christ with Belial?" (2 Corinthians 6:14-15). How can a demon, you, and the Lord walk together in the same company? So "resist the devil, and he will flee from you" (James 4:7).

When mountain walls obstruct thy way,
Why sit and weep? Arise and say,
"Be thou removed!" and they shall be,
By power of God, cast in the sea.

* * *

O'er all the power of fiend or man,
Say to the Lord, "I surely can!"
Take from Him power on earth to tread
On serpent's sting, on dragon's head.[13]

—Joseph Ellison—

Mysteries of Healing

There are mysteries of healing. Every doctor who has been any length of time in general practice will tell you so. I have had the great privilege of having the friendship of a number of good, Christian medical doctors. I think of a great Scottish surgeon in the North of England who, before he used his skillful hands in one of those delicate operations that he performed, would always pray at the operating table, before doctors, students, and nurses, offering his hands for God to use. No wonder that many call him blessed, and thank God for their healing through his surgical skill.

Permit me, if you please, to give some personal experiences. I was once staying in the home of a godly doctor in England whose practice took him to the farms and villages of the dales of Yorkshire. He told me of two significant cases for which he had no answer, but for which he thanked God. He had been tending a hopeless case, a young man sinking fast with a tubercular stomach. He went on visitation to find him dying. The man's mother begged with tears that the doctor should yet do something for him. The doctor knew that all medical skill had come to an end; but in order to pacify her, he gave her a bottle of tablets, with instructions to give the patient one every three hours with water. Neither mother nor patient knew that they were only five-grain aspirin tablets. The next week on his rounds, visiting again the isolated cottages hidden amongst the hills, the doctor called upon his patient, taking with him a death certificate—for by now he knew that the young man would have passed away. To his utter surprise, he was met on the road by his once-dying patient, who was up and about, enjoying his food, and with the first tinges of returning health already upon his features. He became completely well, and testified to the skill and to the wonderful medicine of our good friend the doctor. No special prayer was offered for him, and no hands had been laid upon his head. Both he and his mother were ignorant of the teachings of divine healing. In what category of healing will you put this? I put it under psychosomatic healing.

Again, this same doctor was ministering to another dying patient who had an inoperable condition. No more could be done for her. But, once again, listening to her pleading and moved with compassion, he gave her something for her breast cancer—although he knew that what he gave her could have no effect upon her sad condition. He gave her a bottle of gentian violet,[14] with instructions to dress the open wound with it; and to his utter amazement, there was a complete cure. I call this also psychosomatic healing, that is, healing through psychic forces.

An Example from Bevington's Life

G. C. Bevington, who was born towards the end of the nineteenth century, in his book *Remarkable Incidents and Modern Miracles Through Prayer and Faith*, gives an account of a miracle that can be only divine healing. He was standing upon a chair, reaching towards the ceiling, but stepping too near to the front edge, he turned the chair over and, falling, came down with great force, so that he smashed the chair to pieces and damaged his side so much that he says he could not swallow even water without being thrown into a paroxysm of pain. The doctor x-rayed him and said, "My good man, you are all torn to pieces. Your first rib is separated three fourths of an inch; the second, half; and the third one, about a quarter. There is a sliver torn from your first rib that lays right across your ribs." The kind doctor said that he could get him into a fine hospital in Tennessee, run by his cousin. The cure would take about seven months, but all he would have to pay would be the cost of the artificial ribs. Well, Bevington was not that kind of man. He had a great faith, and he believed most emphatically in divine healing; so he waited upon the Lord. "My suffering seemed to increase," he says,

> *...but I held on.... I saw myself actually sinking down, getting smaller. I could see that I was on the trimming lathe, and was being trimmed down. So I began to praise the Lord.... I kept quietly saying, "Glory! Glory!" At each utterance I could see the shavings a-flying and felt that I was getting the victory. So the "Glorys" would come... louder and louder.... I also saw that what little exertion I had made did not hurt me in the least and as I had not taken a long, down-deep breath for so long, I just wanted to so bad. So I tried it, and oh, what a relief!... Soon I raised my right arm and felt no pain whatever. I then shouted, "O, glory, 'tis done!" I jumped up and began pounding my fractured ribs... A great landslide came into my soul, and I just laughed and shouted and jumped for about three hours.*[15]

He then went to see the doctor and said,

> *"Well, Sir, Doctor, I am a healed man!"... There I was, pounding my ribs, and he was staring wildly at me....*

Then he said, "There must be something in this healing power. I never saw anything like it. And you say that Jesus really healed you without any remedies?"

"Yes, Sir, and now doctor... I would like you to turn the Xray on."

"Oh, I will gladly do it. I am interested in that sliver that lay cross your ribs."

I said, "You will find that splinter in its place."

So when he turned the Xray on, he just stood speechless, while I laughed... he laid his head down on my shoulder, and wept and trembled. I said, "How about that splinter, Doctor?"

He said, "There is no splinter to be seen, and no trace of its ever being there."

And again the glory fell on me and I had to walk the floor. I didn't dare to be too noisy out there in that office...[16]

This is divine healing and, like every healing work of the Lord, it will stand every genuine medical test applied to it, for examination will only demonstrate more fully its authenticity. When Jesus healed a leper, He said to him, "Go thy way, show thyself to the priest" (Mark 1:44), because in those days the priest was the leprosy specialist,[17] and his examination would only confirm the truth of the leper's complete cleansing.

We need the Lord's guidance for each act of faith. He will not work by rote, and God forbid that our acts of faith should only be based on what happened in the past. We pray that He will repeat His works of faith through us, but He will not, of necessity, repeat His methods. We who are children of God live by faith; there is a constant flow of new experiences through which we find that faith is made steadfast. However, we must look each time to the Lord for guidance, and not rely upon what happened in the past. Are you learning this by painful experience?

Examples from Personal Successes & Failures

A number of years ago, I was sitting with my wife in the waiting room of a large children's hospital, because our little daughter was very sick. She had been much prayed for and many had laid hands on her; now, we had liberty from the Lord to take her to the hospital for expert medical advice. I noticed, amongst those waiting there, a woman in the deepest distress, and I was moved by the Spirit to go over and talk to her. I was in clerical attire, so she did not resent, but welcomed, my help. Her little daughter had been taken into the hospital, dying of pneumonia, and there was very little hope. I prayed inwardly and immediately received what Paul calls in 1 Corinthians 12:8 "a word of knowledge." I turned to her and told her that her daughter would completely recover, and that one day she would see me in town when she was with her daughter and tell her, "That is the man who prayed for you and said that God had healed you when you lay dying." Years afterwards I met a gracious, very well-dressed lady, whom at first I had difficulty in recognizing, and who told me with gratitude of her healthy, happy daughter.

I tried to repeat this experience. A deeply distressed couple were brought to the church prayer meeting, and I was told that their child was to have a hole-in-the-heart operation the next day. We enthusiastically prayed, and in wishful thinking, as I now realize it to have been (and with the other case in my mind), I told the couple that all would be well. Afterwards I discovered that I had been sadly misinformed—that the operation had, in fact, taken place that day before we had even held the prayer meeting, and afterwards the child had died. Only my pride was hurt, not God's glory; and I thank my Father for teaching me this lesson.

Divine healing lasts. We do not leave our crutches behind at the great healing meeting in the vast auditorium today, only to have to buy a new set a few months later. When that happens, even though the name of Jesus is used, it is psychic healing.

Many cases of divine healing come to mind to illustrate this. My good friend, George Wood of Manchester, England, was diagnosed by two doctor friends as having inoperable cancer, with three months to live. His condition was confirmed by one of the greatest specialists in England, but he was wonderfully healed, and has lived to testify to healing and heart purity in his own patient, courteous, and persistent way for over twenty more years. I was amongst those who laid hands upon him (a group which also included the two medical doctor friends), in accord with Mark 16:18, when this miracle of healing took place.

Faith works by insistence. I learned, together with my church members, that we could rely upon the inward witness of the Spirit when it was revealed to us that the Lord was present to heal; and deafness, blindness, tuberculosis and pain would yield by our taking our stand and insisting that the thing should go. Following impulse is not the same as being moved by the Spirit, and accomplishes nothing. If you are not sure whether it is the moving of the Spirit or the impulse of your own mind, after waiting upon the Lord, then place it in the hands of the Lord; and if you feel no check, risk it—step out in faith! Too much is left to the healing evangelist. It is time that the children of God realize that they also are called to lay hands upon the sick. If they did so amongst friends and neighbors, many would recover and the healing virtue of the Christ would be made known abroad. Healing will yet be manifested in the streets and homes of our villages and cities as it used to be in the days of the Lord Jesus and of the early church, to the glory of God.

Faith Is For All

We must deal very briefly with a problem that concerns faith, especially for salvation, as it affects not a few. It is the wrong idea, founded upon John 12:39-40, that God reserves faith for some but denies it to others. "Therefore they could not believe, because that Isaiah said, 'He hath blinded their eyes, and hardened their heart.' " (See also Isaiah 6:10.) Of whom is the Holy Spirit speaking in this case? It is of the Jews. "But though He had done so many miracles before them, yet they believed not on Him: that the saying of Isaiah the prophet might be fulfilled" (John 12:37-38). The problem is easily resolved when one sees that it is not the individual Jew who is denied faith, but the Jewish nation. In this very chapter, Jesus calls Jews to believe: "While ye have light, believe in the light, that ye may be the children of light" (John 12:36). Would He have said this if already He had denied them grace to believe? Again He says, "He that believeth on Me, believeth not on Me, but on Him that sent Me... I am come a light into the world, that whosoever believeth on me should not abide in darkness" (verses 44,46). All of the apostles were Jews; most of the early church were Jews; and at Pentecost, three thousand Jews were added to the church. Why did not God allow the Jewish nation to accept the Christ? Because if they had done so, Jesus would have been a king under the Old Covenant, and not a universal Savior under the New Covenant. He had to be rejected by His own so that He could be the Lamb slain, in the will of God, from the foundation of the world.[18] This great truth of God's purpose in preventing the Jewish nation from accepting Jesus as Messiah is the theme of Romans 10-11, where Paul explains that in the end all will be well, for "blindness in part is happened to Israel, until the fulness of the Gentiles be come in. And so all Israel shall be saved" (Romans 11:25-26). This will happen when the Lord Jesus returns the second time, and there will be a great national *Yom Kippur*, that is, Day of Atonement, as Zechariah reveals (Zechariah 12:10-14).

Jesus, confirm my heart's desire
To work, and speak, and think for Thee;
Still let me guard the holy fire,
And still stir up Thy gift in me.

Ready for all Thy perfect will,
My acts of faith and love repeat,
Till death Thy endless mercies seal,
And make the sacrifice complete.[19]

—Charles Wesley—

ENDNOTES FOR CHAPTER 4

---

1. From Tyndale's *Prologues to the Five Books of Moses*
2. Many Christians today have no familiarity with the fourteen books which comprise the Apocrypha. As far back as the days of Jerome (c. 345-420 A.D.), who translated Old and New Testaments into Latin (a work known as the *Vulgate*), these books were not considered canonical (that is, to be included in the list of inspired Scripture); however, they were considered edifying religious literature (much as modern readers look on *Pilgrim's Progress* or *My Utmost for His Highest*). Even after the Roman Catholic Church (which in 1546 at the Council of Trent declared these Apocryphal books canonical, anathematizing anyone who didn't accept them as such) and the Protestant Reformation parted ways on the inspiration of these books, Protestant publishing houses

usually bound the Apocryphal books between the Old and New Testaments. This was probably true of the Bibles used by Bunyan and Whitefield in the examples Pastor Gutteridge cites.

3. Ecclesiasticus (not to be confused with the canonical book *Ecclesiastes*) is also called *The Wisdom of Jesus the Son of Sirach* or simply *Sirach.*
4. From Bunyan's autobiography, *Grace Abounding to the Chief of Sinners*, paragraphs 62-65.
5. 1 Maccabees 4:24
6. The citation is from *The Journals of George Whitefield.*
7. The allusion is to John 10:27.
8. Albert Benjamin Simpson (1843-1919), a Canadian minister, was the founder of the Christian & Missionary Alliance. He emphasized healing as a part of the Fourfold Gospel he preached: "Jesus our Savior, Sanctifier, Healer, and Coming King." Simpson and the C&MA had a strong influence on early Pentecostalism.
9. Charles Sydney Price (1887-1947) was a Pentecostal evangelist, and numerous miraculous healings that occurred in his meetings became well publicized.
10. The allusion is to John 9:4 (with a nod towards John 6:28).
11. See comments on Ecclesiastes 10:10 in Matthew Henry's *Commentary on the Whole Bible.*
12. The allusion is to the story of the "prodigal son" in Luke 15:11-32.
13. From Ellison's poem "Be Thou Removed" in his book *The Anointed Life* (Northampton: D. Arnold & Co.; 1935). See the appendix, page 187, for the full poem.
14. *Gentian violet*—a simple topical, antifungal agent
15. G. C. Bevington, *Remarkable Incidents and Modern Miracles Through Prayer and Faith*, pages 109-11
16. Bevington, pages 111-112
17. Leviticus 13 and 14
18. The allusion is to Revelation 13:8.

19. From Wesley's ***O Thou Who Camest from Above***. The full context can be read in the appendix on page 188.

·5·
The Perfecting of Faith

The Major Obstacle to Faith

GOD IS VERY DILIGENT TO MAKE our faith perfect. Paul prays exceedingly, night and day, that he might see the Thessalonians face to face and perfect what was lacking in their faith (1 Thessalonians 3:10).

The major obstacle to faith is sin. Sin brings a barrier between us and God, so that faith cannot operate. Healing can be frustrated by sin. Harmony in the body is health. Disharmony in the body, which is disease, can often be traced to disharmony in the soul caused by refusal to walk in revealed light. *"Your iniquities have separated between you and your God, and your sins have hid His face from you, that He will not hear"* (Isaiah 59:2). It is rarely open sin that hinders faith; one who is living openly in disobedience to God is not concerned about the exercise of true faith; it is hidden sin that causes the trouble.

Very often the hindrance is an unforgiving spirit (Mark 11:25-26). Even from a physiological point of view, a rankling, unforgiving spirit causes a fester in the mind that will manifest itself physically in the disease of the body. The very word "disease" means "apart from" or to be "deprived of ease." Very often the Lord links healing with forgiveness of sin. Remember that He has promised forgiveness only to those who forgive. "But if ye forgive not men their trespasses, neither will your Father forgive your trespasses" (Matthew 6:15). The Psalmist says, "Bless the Lord, O my soul, and forget not all His benefits: Who forgiveth all thine iniquities; Who healeth all thy diseases" (Psalm 103:2,3). Jesus said first to the sick of the palsy, "Son, thy sins be forgiven thee," and later, "Arise and take up thy bed" (Mark 2:5,9).

The Perfecting of Character

Understand, however, that there are other reasons for sickness besides sin. The history of Job demonstrates this. God testified that His servant Job was "a perfect and an upright man" (Job 1:8), and despite this, Job suffered from a grievous sickness. It was permitted as chastisement, that Job might be a partaker of God's holiness. It is a Bible demonstration of the truth that a perfect heart is the only foundation for a perfect character. The first—the perfect heart—is *given*; the second—the perfect character—has to be *forged*. But the first is the first, and must come before the second, a simple fact of arithmetic that has not yet been learned by many Christians. "Blessed is the man whom Thou chasteneth, O Lord" (Psalm 94:12); therefore, let no one say in his folly that the Christian who is sick must, of necessity, be guilty of sin. This is very wrong teaching. Epaphroditus (Philippians 2:25-27), Trophimus (2 Timothy 4:20b), and Timothy (1 Timothy 5:23) rise up to contradict this. Such teachers "talk to the grief of those whom Thou hast wounded" (Psalm 69:26).

The State of the Heart

This book is not a treatise on sanctification, nor will it be allowed to develop into such. Nevertheless, one cannot deal with the great subject of the perfecting of faith without making mention of the cause of most of our troubles preventing the exercise of faith, which is our state of heart. The Bible teaching upon the heart makes it the center of both *will* and *emotion.* "With the heart man believeth unto righteousness" (Romans 10:10). That is the operation, by grace, of the *will.* "I sleep, but my heart waketh; it is the voice of my beloved" (Song of Solomon 5:2)—that is the quickening of *emotion.* Any act is either right or wrong according to the motive in doing it (that is, morally right or wrong, for an act may result in unpleasant consequences without the motive having been evil). What is the underlying state of a responsible human being's heart? "The heart is deceitful above all things and desperately wicked: who can know it?" (Jeremiah 17:9) This is the state of a cultured, refined, well-educated, unregenerate person's heart. It is also the state of an uncultured, unrefined, ill-educated, unregenerate person's heart —"for there is no difference: for all have sinned" (Romans 3:22-23). It is impossible to discern adequately the intentions of the heart—that inheritance of our Adamic nature. It doubles and turns and twists. The first great necessity is to get one's motives ordered and right, and most importantly, to see that, whereas no human being can discern the motives of the heart, there is One who can. Let us continue with Jeremiah's word, "Who can know it? I, the LORD search the heart!" (Jeremiah 17:9-10) So there is One who can plumb the human heart to its deepest depths—"I, the LORD!" In regeneration, that is, the new birth (which is the major work that the Holy Spirit performs in man), God both cleanses and renews. He potentially cleanses the human heart—the fountain of the soul—and at the same instant gives a new heart, which is the heart of the new man in Christ.

Hearts Purified by Faith

This was the experience of Cornelius, recorded in Acts 15. Peter confuted the arguments of the Judaeans (who said that circumcision and the keeping of the law of Moses was also a condition of salvation) by pointing out that uncircumcised Gentiles had had their hearts purified, not by conformity to law, but by their faith. Peter confirmed the word of Jeremiah, as referred to above, by saying, "God which knoweth the heart bare them witness" (verse 8). Because of their honest desire for truth, the Lord had given them grace to believe in Jesus. They exercised the faith granted to them, and He witnessed to their act of faith by giving them the Holy Spirit, who, when He came in, purified their hearts. This is in complete conformity to what Peter had proclaimed to the Jews at Pentecost: "Repent, and be baptized every one of you in the name of Jesus Christ, for the remission of sins, and ye shall receive the gift of the Holy Ghost" (Acts 2:38). Water baptism is a desirable, outward demonstration of repentance toward Christ by the one believing, but it is not a necessity to that great salvation which, under the New Covenant, includes the gift of the Holy Spirit. This is proven by the fact that the Gentiles, with Cornelius, were baptized after they had received the Holy Spirit in salvation, and not before (Acts 10:47).

Once the heart—from which "evil thoughts, murders, adulteries, fornications, thefts, false witness, blasphemies" proceed (as Jesus says in Matthew 15:19)—has been purified, the *act* of faith which procured that pure heart from God must become a *state* of faith. Allow the Holy Spirit to keep the heart clean, by instantly confessing to God any fault that He reveals. Jesus said to His disciples, "He that is washed needeth not save to wash his feet, but is clean every whit" (John 13:10).

O may the least omission pain
My well-instructed soul,
And drive me to the blood again
Which makes the wounded whole![1]

—Charles Wesley—

Naaman's Cleansing: A Type

The great truth that the Lord will cleanse the hidden man of the heart is beautifully revealed in the history of Naaman. Once more let us turn back to this story and see how, under the Bible figure of deliverance from leprosy, God cleanses the heart. Deliverance from leprosy is not a figure of forgiveness for past *acts* of sin, but of cleansing from the *state* of sin. Naaman, the leper, would have taken a very poor view of the teaching of one of our modern, antinomian fundamentalists, who would have assured him that although his state was very shocking, yet his standing was quite all right. Scripture knows nothing of this playing on words. This wrong doctrine has the unhappy result of justifying the sinful condition of many church members who have not been taught the truth that "whosoever abideth in Him sinneth not" and "he that doeth righteousness is righteous" (1 John 3:6-7). Naaman is given, in Scripture, this testimony: "a great man with his master, and honourable... he was also a mighty man in valour, but he was a leper" (2 Kings 5:1). That just about sums up most members of Congress in the United States and members of the Houses of Parliament in Great Britain and some other countries: fine people in every other way, but sinners. There is coming a time when the saints of the Most High (we hope that many of the aforementioned will be amongst them) shall possess the Kingdom (Daniel 7:22)—men and women of perfect heart, who shall rule with perfect justice out of perfect love, in the confidence of perfect faith.

Look again at the Naaman chapter (2 Kings 5), and see what his seven dips were for. They were for:

1. Anger—(verses 11,12);

2. The ruling "I"—(verse 11);

3. Unbelief—*his* God, not *my* God—(verse 11);

4. Pride—chariots and horses—(verse 9); and—"he will surely come out to me" (verse 11);

5. His own way and works—"took with him ten talents of silver" (verse 5);

6. Love of this world—Abana and Pharpar better than all the waters of Israel—(verse 12); and, finally,

7. Idolatry—(verse 18).

Did Naaman's cleansing change Naaman in these things? Was it only the flesh that the Lord dealt with? Was He not more concerned about the heart? Look at your Bible again:

1. Where has Naaman's *anger* gone? For Elisha said, "Go in peace" (verse 19).

2. What has happened to that dominant and ruling *"I"*? For three times Naaman says "thy *servant*" (verses 15,17-18).

3. What of his previous *unbelief*? For after his cleansing he says, "Now I *know*" (verse 15).

4. Where is his *pride* that made him stand in his chariot before the door of Elisha's hut? It has gone, and now he returns and stands before Elisha a humble, thankful man. See also how he alighted from that same chariot to serve the servant of Elisha (verse 21).

5. What will he now say of cleansing *by his own works*? His flesh has come again like that of a little child (verses 14), for the attitude of a little child is the Lord's condition for salvation (Matthew 18:3).

6. Will he now *love this world*? Will Syria be sweeter to him than the land of Jehovah? Not now! He begs for two

mules' burdens of the earth of the land of Israel, so that he might have an altar unto the true God in his own land (2 Kings 5:17 and Exodus 20:24).

7. As for *idolatry*, from henceforth he will "offer neither burnt offering nor sacrifice unto other gods, but only unto the LORD" (2 Kings 5:17).

Naaman came to Elisha with a little faith, a mixed faith; otherwise he would not have come at all. But he went back with a pure faith. The Lord is willing to perfect what is lacking in our faith as well.

Stages of Faith

There are three most important stages in the faith of the believer, and because this is not recognized, many a contest of faith is lost. Faith is a mountain to be climbed.

1. The first position up the mountainside is one that all true Christians take. We may phrase it thus: "I believe that God *can* do the thing that I am asking Him to do."

2. The next plateau to be climbed is that upon which I can stand and declare that God *will* do this thing.

3. The final struggle up the mountain to the peak ends when I announce that the thing is *done*—God has performed it. I have the *assurance* that He has heard, and although I see it not, yet I know that I have the petition that I desired of Him (1 John 5:15).

If I have only the faith of stage one, then it will not operate that of stage two; or if I have the faith of stage two, then it will not bring the triumph of the mountain peak where, like our God, we call "those things which be not as though they were"

(Romans 4:17), and prove ourselves true sons of faithful Abraham.

Faith, Hope, and Love: The Bethany Family

Faith cannot exist separately from Hope and Love. Although the Holy Spirit may, at present, be concentrating in your life upon faith, in order to prepare you for the fight against the unbelieving forces of this age, He is by no means neglectful of hope and love. All three are most necessary bastions of the Kingdom of God, and He is perfecting the saint by perfecting these in him. This is what the Lord was doing when He raised Lazarus from the dead. To rightly understand this miracle, we have to see who the characters mentioned in John 11 represent. God's unit throughout all of His creation is the family; this must be so, for His most wonderful and worthy name is "Father"—a special revelation to the heirs of the New Covenant. Whether it is the inconceivably small atom, with its electrons around the nucleus, or the awe-inspiring immensity of a galaxy, which is a vast assembly of stars with their solar systems, each has been created upon the family principle. Man has been honored in a way that angels have never been, by being permitted upon earth to form a family of his own—something that certain angels envied and sinned in copying (we shall refer to this later)—for in the other world there is neither marrying nor giving in marriage, as the Lord Jesus revealed (Matthew 22:30). Jesus loves the family and seeks to heal it; the evil one hates it and ever seeks to destroy it. Hence the divorces and broken homes of these degenerate days.

There was trouble in the Bethany family where Jesus loved to be. There were rest, and sympathy, and love for Him in the home of Martha, Lazarus and Mary, but sickness had come in, and Lazarus was very ill and lay dying. The Lord Jesus is perfect in everything: "As for God, His way is perfect... and... He maketh my way perfect" (Psalm 18:30,32). This sickness had not come without His design and permission. He had planned to perfect Martha, Lazarus and Mary. Now these three are God's demonstration, in human form, of His great qualities of Faith and Hope and Love. Martha represents faith; Lazarus is hope; and Mary is love.

Faith brings rest and peace; hope produces courage and patience; love gives joy. Hope always looks to the future and believes in it; that is why the blessed hope of the Church is the future coming of the Lord Jesus Christ and the resurrection of the holy dead. Since Lazarus is hope, he must inevitably rise from the dead. Martha, being God's picture of faith, must always be active, doing something. Faith always works. If it is not working, it is dead. Paul says, "Remembering without ceasing your work of faith" (1 Thessalonians 1:3), and again he speaks of being offered "upon the sacrifice and service of your faith" (Philippians 2:17). Poor Martha, like real faith itself, is so greatly misunderstood. How many preachers have you heard depreciating Martha in order to magnify Mary? It is like depreciating faith in order to enhance love. Let both stand! Of course Martha is always working! What else should faith be doing?

All the Marys in the Gospels reveal love. Mary the Mother of Jesus is suffering love; Mary Magdalene is repentant love; and Mary of Bethany is adoring love. Hope, however, is sick; there is no confidence in the future; he sinks, and the home is filled with gloomy forebodings. He dies, and the light fades; night has come to the home where it seemed that once the sun was always shining. If you look at this chapter, you will find that the order of their names has gone wrong. There is always a right order for things. God's order is Faith, Hope, Love, as Paul makes clear in his first letter to the saints at Corinth: "Now there abideth faith, hope and love" (1 Corinthians 13:13). But look at the order in the chapter that we are considering (John 11). It is wrong in verse one, because the order is hope (Lazarus), love (Mary), faith (Martha); and in verse 5, it is *faith, love, hope.* This is indicative of sickness somewhere; hope has gone wrong, and it has spread to faith and love.

Now, Jesus is revealed as perfect faith and hope and love in this chapter. See His perfection of faith when He says to the Father, "I thank Thee that Thou hast heard Me. And I knew that Thou hearest Me always" (verses 41-42). He is perfect hope: He has perfect confidence for the future—all will take place according to His will, even though at present all seems contrary. So when He heard that Lazarus was sick, "He abode two days still in the same place where He was" (verse 6) and let Lazarus die! What of His love? Was there ever love like His? He had gone away from Judea into the place beyond Jordan where once John had baptized, because the Jews had sought to stone Him, but He had escaped out of their hands (John 10:31, 39-40). Nevertheless, He had not ceased to love these Jews; so, from afar, He permitted Lazarus to be sick and die, that He might do a double deed: perfect the family at Bethany, and by showing the antagonistic Jews a mighty miracle, prove to them that His claims were just. Did He not say, "This sickness is not unto death, but for the glory of God, that the Son of God might be glorified thereby" (verse 4)? After His mighty miracle of raising a dead, decayed, and corrupt body into immediate radiant health, "many of the Jews which came to Mary, and had seen the things that Jesus did, believed on Him" (verse 45).

Now see how this spiritual sickness has also infected Jesus' disciples. Jesus loves them, and us, too, and longs to perfect all faith and hope and love, for nothing less than our perfection will ever please Him. Also, He will only tolerate His own divine order. How did you come into the new birth? Did not grace first give you faith, so that down the channel of faith God might send His Holy Spirit in order that you should be born from above? What did faith do then? It birthed in you "a lively [living] hope" (1 Peter 1:3), and finally, "hope maketh not ashamed; because the love of God is shed abroad in our hearts by the Holy Ghost which is given unto us" (Romans 5:5). The disciples' faith is lacking. Jesus said, "I am glad for your sakes that I was not there, to the intent ye may believe" (John 11:15). Hope is lacking, too. Listen to cheerful Thomas! "Let us also go, that we may die with Him" (verse 16). As for their love, we are filled with shame for them (and conviction, too). How often had thirteen hungry men descended upon Lazarus for a meal and a night's lodging! Now, when Jesus decides to return to Bethany in response to the request of Martha and Mary, the disciples remember the attempted stoning and say, "Master, the Jews of late sought to stone Thee; and goest Thou thither again?" (verse 8) It seems that in view of a possible shower of stones, they would prefer that Mary and Martha look after their own troubles.

But see the complete absence of faith, hope, and love in the kingdom of Satan, and observe the opposite qualities ruling in their stead. The chief priests and Pharisees were of their father, the devil, said Jesus (John 8:44). There is no faith, but antagonistic doubt: "If we let Him thus alone, all men will believe on Him" (John 11:48). There is no hope, but despair: "The Romans shall come and take away both our place and nation" (verse 48). There is no love, but hate: "They took counsel together for to put Him to death" (verse 53).

Now Jesus comes, and as ever, faith is always first. "Then Martha, as soon as she heard that Jesus was coming, went and met Him" (verse 20). See the wonder of her faith! Wounded it is, but still vigorous. Hope is dead, but it will revive if only faith lives. Hear this beautiful character, Martha! Her brother Lazarus is dead, but she still proclaims her faith in the Christ. She says,

"Lord, if Thou hadst been here, my brother had not died. But I know that even now, whatsoever Thou wilt ask of God, God will give it Thee" (verse 22). Is not that one of the most wonderful declarations of faith in the whole Bible? But she has not finished; listen to her again! "I know that he shall rise again in the resurrection at the last day" (verse 24). That is good, but it is not perfect, for she does not say "now," but "in the last day." That kind of faith is like the plateau just short of the mountain peak that we mentioned previously. It says, "I know that the Lord will"; but it cannot raise Lazarus from the dead. Jesus says to her, "I am the resurrection, and the life: he that believeth in Me, though he were dead, yet shall he live... believest thou...?" (verses 25-26) Faith then climbs to the mountain peak. She says, "Yea, Lord: I believe that Thou art the Christ, the Son of God" (verse 7). After that, Jesus can go on to raise Lazarus from the dead because, believing that He is the Christ and the Resurrection, Martha has come to the great epitome of faith: "I believe that He does do it," and in vision, she could see her brother coming out of the tomb.

Mary, wounded love, "sat still in the house" (verse 20), but hearing that Jesus was calling for her, "she arose quickly" (verse 29) and came to Jesus. Faith will walk, but love must run! It was Mary's love that moved Jesus' compassion and brought down His tears. Lazarus now is raised from the dead and all is well. We will leave the restored family. The Gospel makes it clear that all is now in the right order (John 12:2-3). It is Martha, Lazarus, and Mary—that is, Faith, Hope and Love—all abiding in the home with Jesus. "There they made Him a supper and Martha served"—as ever, standing, as faith always does, waiting on work and service. "Lazarus was one of them that sat at the table with Him." That is perfect and right; hope sits restful and in peace, communing with Jesus and waiting in patience. "Then took Mary a pound of ointment of spikenard, very costly, and anointed the feet of Jesus" (verse 3). This is the place of love—at

His feet, in adoring union with Him. So there "abideth faith, hope, charity [love], these three; but the greatest of these is charity [love]. Follow after love" (1 Corinthians 13:13—14:1); or, as Jesus says, "Mary has chosen that good part, which shall not be taken away from her" (Luke 10:42).

In the past, too unbelieving
'Midst the tempest I have been,
And my heart has slowly trusted
What my eyes have never seen.
Blessèd Jesus, teach me on Thine arm to lean.

O for trust that brings me triumph
When defeat seems strangely near!
O for faith that changes fighting
Into Vict'ry's ringing cheer!
Faith triumphant! Knowing not defeat or fear.[2]

—Herbert Booth—

ENDNOTES FOR CHAPTER 5

1. From the hymn ***I Want a Principle Within***, all the stanzas of which may be found on page 189.
2. Booth's complete hymn, ***Blessèd Lord, in Thee Is Refuge***, is given on page 190.

·6·

The Life and Growth of Faith

Faith-Life

LIFE IS THE GREATEST OF ALL human desires. Even most suicides rush out of this life because they think that the next life cannot be as unpleasant as the one which they are now enduring. When Graceless in *Pilgrim's Progress* was convinced that the City of Destruction, in which he dwelt, was going to fall into Tophet,[1] "the man put his fingers in his ears and ran on, crying, 'Life! Eternal life!' " Because of this, his name was changed to *Christian*. The Lord Jesus said, "I am come that they might have life, and that they might have it more abundantly" (John 10:10).

This life, the life of God, is not an added stimulus to the old one. The Lord Jesus does not add a piece of new cloth to an old garment (Matthew 9:16,17). A weaver well knows what He means. Freshly woven cloth, known as "grey cloth" in the industry, must not be added to material that has already been shrunk, bleached, and dyed. If a piece of "undressed cloth" (original word) is used for such a purpose, when the garment is washed the new cloth will shrink and pull away from the other material. What the Lord is indicating is that His kind of life is narrower than that of this world.

It is the same message, but in a different metaphor, when He speaks of entering into life through the strait gate into the narrow way. Your heavenly life, with its new and deeper faith, is too *narrow* for those who only know the earthly one. Even some of the best people will censure your faith. The disciples once said to Jesus, "Knowest Thou that the Pharisees were offended?" Jesus answered, "Let them alone!" (Matthew 15:12-14) You let them alone, too!

Paradoxically, your new faith-life is much too *big* for these same people; you have become exceedingly fanatical to them. The Lord Jesus warns you of this also, when in the same scripture He says, "Neither do men put new wine into old bottles [*wineskins*, and so throughout the passage] else the bottles break and the wine runneth out, and the bottles perish: but they put new wine into new bottles, and both are preserved" (Matthew 9:17). The life of faith is too narrow, and too expansive, for this world. There is a reproach in this new life, but faith must not be a sneak; it puts out its hand to touch the hem of Jesus' garment, even though disapproving religious people are looking on (Luke 8:43-48).

How Abraham Learned Faith: Steps of Obedience

We are always learning lessons from Abraham. Paul tells us that we are to "walk in the steps of that faith of our father Abraham" (Romans 4:12). Abraham did not learn his faith all at once; he walked one step at a time. His first step was to leave Ur of the Chaldees (the idolaters' city) with his father Terah. This began his life of faith. After a journey of a thousand miles, along the Euphrates to Charan, he was called to his second step—to Canaan. He did not arrive in Canaan all at once, nor did the children of Israel. Their first step was through the Red Sea into the wilderness; their second was over Jordan into the Promised Land. You will probably have to do the same thing. Very few step from Egypt into Canaan; they usually have to put in some time in the desert before the life of faith is established. ***Abram***, which means "high father," became ***Abraham***—"father of a multitude"—only because he walked in obedience to God. Every promise of God is also a command. Conversely, every command contains a promise. The first lesson which we learn from Abraham, then, is to be obedient. Obedience will always bring the reward.

Faith is almost synonymous with obedience. Abraham "staggered not at the promise of God through unbelief; but was strong in faith, giving glory to God" (Romans 4:20). This was when the Lord had promised him a son when he was past age. He staggered not then, because he staggered not when God first called him out. If he had staggered on the Charan road or on the last lap of the journey to Canaan, he would then have staggered when he was faced with greater promises. A man hit by an arrow staggers and falls. Doubts are the devil's arrows. Abraham did not indulge himself in the luxury of doubting; he held aloft the shield of faith (Ephesians 6:16). Not one of the arrows of unbelief hit him; thus "he staggered not through unbelief."

You will always be led on, step by step, to greater, higher steps of faith. An adult chamois,[2] five thousand feet up among the rocks, can leap from pinnacle to pinnacle, where the foothold is but the size of an English crown piece or an American silver dollar. It could not have done this when only a few days old; it had to start to balance on a tiny height which had a broader platform. I have held my breath as I have seen the baby lambs skipping from rock to rock high up on the mountains of Wales. I have also seen their dead bodies at the foot of a precipice. These were presumptuous, and were out of reach of the shepherd. Also, they had not learned obedience. "Thou standest by faith. Be not highminded, but fear" (Romans 11:20). You are watched over by the Good Shepherd, who "when He putteth forth His own sheep, He goeth before them, and the sheep follow Him" (John 10:4); so you are perfectly safe if you will obey and follow. "Follow" means "come after," not "go before."

Not His Own Faith

Paul also says that Abraham was "the father of us all—before Him whom he believed" (Romans 4:16-17); but the marginal rendering is more significant: ***"Like unto Him whom he believed."*** He was like to God in his faith; he did not use his own faith, but the faith that God gave to him. Abraham was not an extraordinary man; he was just an ordinary man believing in an extraordinary Person, the Living God. Abraham never performed a miracle, but God was always doing signs and wonders for him. Abraham's life was full of visions, theophanies,[3] prophecies, manifestations, victories, and miracles; but all that Abraham really did was to obey and go on believing God. Will you ask the Lord to teach you Abraham's walk of faith, which is the operation of *the faith of the Son of God*? Let the Lord Jesus then operate His faith through you.

Dr. A. B. Simpson wrote of a copperplate engraving that, examined at reading distance, was a copy of the American Constitution, but held at arm's length, revealed a wonderful likeness of George Washington—so cleverly had it been written and arranged. The Bible is like that engraving—its words are meant to reveal the Truth, that is, ***Christ***, of whom the Bible is but a revelation. "And beginning at Moses and all the prophets, He expounded unto them in all the scriptures the things concerning Himself" (Luke 24:27). All is Christ and Christ is all. Having Him, you have all things—a boundless store of faith for today and for every tomorrow, with all the unknown needs and conflicts.

They who know the Saviour shall in Him be strong,
Mighty in the conflict of the right 'gainst wrong.
This the blessèd promise given in God's Word,
Doing wondrous exploits, they who know the Lord.

Chorus:
Victory! victory! blessèd blood-bought victory,
Victory! victory! vict'ry all the time!
As Jehovah liveth, strength divine He giveth
Unto those who know Him, vict'ry all the time!

In the midst of battle, be not thou dismayed,
Tho' the powers of darkness 'gainst thee are arrayed;
God, thy strength, is with thee, causing thee to stand,
Heaven's allied armies wait at thy command.

Brave to bear life's testing, strong the foe to meet,
Walking like a hero midst the furnace heat,
Doing wondrous exploits with the Spirit's sword,
Winning souls for Jesus; praise, O praise the Lord![4]

—Mrs. C. H. Morris—

You are not going to be deluded, for what He calls you to believe is true; count on His faithfulness. He calls you to have faith, and the One who does so "is faithful that promised" (Hebrews 10:23). The centurion said, "Speak the word only, and my servant shall be healed" (Matthew 8:8). He was "like unto God"; he could count the things that are not as though they were. And Jesus said, "I have not found so great faith, no, not in Israel" (Matthew 8:10).

Growth in Maturity

All earthly life grows toward maturity. This is also true of life in the Spirit, but with this difference—spiritual life is always becoming mature only to commence another phase of maturity. This will go on through all eternity. Paul commends the Thessalonians because "your faith groweth exceedingly" (2 Thessalonians 1:3). The divine tree of faith has been planted in good and fruitful soil; now, provided that the conditions for growth are kept right, Paul is satisfied that the tree will bud and leaf and blossom and bear fruit with ever-increasing measure, forever.

The Lord Jesus Christ, by whom are all things and for whom are all things, knows all that there is to know about horticulture. Had you forgotten for a moment that He invented it? "All things were made by Him; and without Him was not anything made that was made" (John 1:3). He wants you to be well instructed in this most important subject of fruitful faith, so He says, "Consider the lilies of the field, how they grow" (Matthew 6:28). The emphasis in the verse is on the word ***how***; let us therefore consider, without wandering down the paths of botany or biology, how plants grow. This is a book on faith, so do not expect a treatise on photosynthesis or the process of osmosis (which were, however, both originated by the Lord Jesus and are great necessities in the life and growth of plants).

Effort and Rest

But we will deal with more simple things. How do plants grow? By alternate effort and rest. So important is the rest period that God created the earth with a necessity for rest. He rested Himself from creating, and made for us a sabbath rest of one day in seven. More than this, He instituted a one year's rest in seven for the soil, when it could recover its strength by lying fallow. Much of earth's sickness is caused by greedy, unbelieving man denying to the earth its proper rest. Our harvests would be more plentiful and our food more wholesome if we obeyed God. (See Leviticus 25:1-6 and 2 Chronicles 36:21.) This is more clearly seen when one realizes that God has provided a rest period through autumn and winter, with revival in spring and full growth in summer—then rest again.

Effort and rest are even more evident in the opening of a bud, the emergence of an *imago*[5] from its nymph state in the metamorphosis of an insect, or the breaking out of a chick from an egg. The only way, of course, to see the opening of a bud is by means of time-lapse photography, where a film has been taken over many hours and then greatly speeded up. But anyone may watch a butterfly emerging from its chrysalis; or, easier still, see a baby chicken coming out of the egg. In every case, there is a strong, impulsive effort, followed by a time of inertia, of quiet rest. This is God's way of growth for lilies—and men. You will not be called to a continual effort of extraordinary faith, but to a succession of periods of special times of faith, and then to rest.

Retaining the Ground Won

Nevertheless, to change the metaphor—the ground won must be retained. The plateau gained is a camping site to provide a base for a higher climb up the mountainside; so it is in a life of faith, all the time. The Lord would have you to be without anxiety. A lily grows in simple faith; so, if you discover that you have been put on one side for a time, still believe! It is a time for consolidation of ground won, in preparation for claiming further territory ahead. Those who do not know these simple rules of growth in faith will tell you that you are backslidden, and would have you begin a perilous time of heart-searching for secret sin. It is very dangerous to keep company with that lying jade "introspection"; she usually haunts the steps of those who long to walk closely with their Lord. This attitude of searching one's own heart is against faith. The Lord is the only true searcher of the heart, for He alone knows it, and He has promised to reveal to us anything there that displeases Him.

"And if in anything ye be otherwise minded, God shall reveal even this unto you" (Philippians 3:15). Again, "thine ears shall hear a word behind thee, saying, 'This is the way, walk ye in it,' when ye turn to the right hand, and when ye turn to the left" (Isaiah 30:21). Those who are the Lord's sheep will hear and know His voice, and will have no need to be anxious lest their ways are displeasing to the Shepherd. Faith has confidence in Him that He will, by His indwelling Spirit, reveal all faults as we walk in the light. This is one of the privileges of the rest of faith.

Faith has its delays, which are all a part of the work of faith. After the Lord Jesus had cursed the barren fig tree (Mark 11:12-14), the disciples saw no immediate difference, for there was none apparent to the eye. However, the almighty Word had spoken—the same Word that had originally said, "Let the earth bring forth... the fruit tree yielding fruit" (Genesis 1:11). The Word was now commanding the reverse, and the destroying work had instantly begun. The Lord Jesus passed calmly on. The disciples may have foolishly thought that this was an indignant word spoken, a word of annoyance because He was hungry; but they did not then know the Lord. They were astonished when, upon their return, they found that the fig tree had dried up from the roots. It was a demonstration to them that God expects fruit from those whom He has created to produce it, as Jesus taught His disciples later when He said, "I am the true vine and My Father is the husbandman; every branch in Me that beareth not fruit He taketh away" (John 15:1,2). It was also a solemn warning to the "fig-tree" nation—the Jews—that because of their sin, they would be dried up. We must not expect instantaneous action unless it is necessary. So many believe and look, see nothing, and doubt. **True faith swamps the doubts with "I believe."**

Faith is a hidden thing; it is like a grain of mustard seed that one hides away in the earth. The sower must have faith to believe that there is growth, although it may be hidden. "Be patient therefore, brethren... Behold, the husbandman waiteth for the precious fruit of the earth and hath long patience for it.... Be ye also patient" (James 5:7,8). The man who continually digs his seed up to see how it is getting on will have no harvest. So, speak the word of faith and believe; then in due time the work of faith will be revealed, for "blessed are they that have not seen and yet have believed" (John 20:29). Restless unbelief kills the seed; an agitated spirit looking for signs of growth is not operating the faith of God.

Faith Comes by Hearing

The great necessity in all this is to have received a word from God; an act of faith must always be the product of a divinely given word. We have already pointed out—but it must be repeated again and again—that faith cometh by hearing (so are you listening?) and "hearing by the Word of God" (Romans 10:17). That is, not just words that God once said to someone else under other circumstances, or even under similar ones to your own at some time in the past (as recorded in the Bible), but a word that He is saying personally to you now!

Because there is such a dearth of men and women who are walking with God at this time, the teaching is usually given that one may take one's own word from the Scriptures: "Every promise in the book is yours, and there are over five thousand promises in the Bible," and so on. I have found that when I have been counseling a Christian in need, and I have asked him, "Has the Lord given you a word?" the reply almost invariably is, "What do you mean by the Lord giving me a word?" They have been taught to believe that the word of the Lord—"My sheep hear My voice" (John 10:27)—means that they should read and memorize the Bible, but nothing more than that. It takes time to receive the word of the Lord; He speaks at His time, in His will, not ours. It is much quicker, in this hour of rush and shortcuts, to fly to the "promise box" with its heterogeneous collection of pleasant scripture texts.

The Rest of Faith

We have made a brief mention of the rest of faith, but it is such an important part of the life and growth of faith that we must have a closer look at it. The rest of faith is not the enjoyment of *future* Paradise, but a *present* breathing of the atmosphere of Heaven. It is an **abiding in a deep-settled peace, which is at the very root of the life of faith**, even though storms of adversity and persecution, with waves of trouble and conflict, are going over the head. It is of the mind, the attitude and the very nature of Jesus; it is peace flowing like a river; it is righteousness as certain, as progressive, as abundant, as ceaseless as the waves of the ocean. It is God's full purpose in creating man. Adam and Eve had a great measure of it while they were in the Garden of Eden.

This rest is the complete opposite of that which sin generates in the fallen nature. The rest of faith is like Lazarus—the one-time beggar—now in Abraham's bosom, above the great gulf under which lies the selfish, once-rich man, "Dives,"[6] who is restless, tormented, and unsatisfied (Luke 16:19-31), because "the wicked are like the troubled sea, when it cannot rest, whose waters cast up mire and dirt. There is no peace... to the wicked" (Isaiah 57:20,21). No unregenerate human being can enjoy the rest of faith, because it is of the peace of God. No psychiatric treatment can ever bring it, because all that the sincere psychiatrist can do is to work with the material he has in hand, which is the limited human mind; and what we are considering is "the peace of God which passeth all understanding" (Philippians 4:7). This is a rest that is only "for the people of God" (Hebrews 4:9). "Be zealous therefore," says the writer of Hebrews, "to enter into that rest" (Hebrews 4:11). It cannot be entered into by just assenting to the truth of the Scriptures about faith, but only by allowing the Lord to bring one to the place of faith by His chastening. It is always true "that we must through much tribulation enter into the kingdom of God" (Acts 14:22). Those who, with Job, are willing to say to their Beloved, "Though He slay me, yet will I trust in Him" (Job 13:15), and who, without complaining—but perhaps often with tears and sighing—still look up to and trust in Him, will be brought at last to the place of faith where they will enter into His rest. There is no other way.

In this life of faith, what does the rest of faith effect? The greatest thing is that it pleases God. We were made for Him, and it is "His rest" that we enter into. It begets in us a constancy, a nobility of character that is like Jesus: so gentle and yet so strong; completely pliable and yet absolutely unbreakable; dignified and yet humble. He was taken captive and led to the slaughter as unresisting as a lamb, but He could not be compelled to speak a word. The one who has entered into this rest of faith ***knows***, not just "assumes" or "makes an effort to believe," that his "old man is crucified with Christ." The slightest variance with the way of the Spirit, or any conduct that is of the nature of sin, is instantly recognized, because of the check of the Spirit, and is confessed, pardoned, and cleansed because of the ever-prevailing Blood of the everlasting covenant that abides upon the child of God. Even such momentary transgressions are utilized to enter more deeply into the rest of faith. The reliance upon the Father's word that He forgives upon confession, the loving acceptance of His forgiveness, the refusal to think upon the wrong act or thought, makes even the lapse a means of grace to establish the soul in oneness with God.

What of others' sin? We are grieved for them, but we do not allow it to disturb the peace of God. "Fret not thyself because of evildoers" (Psalm 37:1) is the gracious enabling command of our Father, who also adds:

- "Trust in the LORD" (verse 3);
- "Delight thyself also in the LORD" (verse 4);
- "Commit thy way unto the LORD" (verse 5);
- "Rest in the LORD" (verse 7), for "the meek shall inherit the earth and delight themselves in the abundance of peace" (verse 11).

"Mark the perfect man, and behold the upright: for the end of that man is peace" (verse 37). The Most High regards all the evil of all the earth; does He fret?

Brother Lawrence, who was a lay brother in the Carmelite Monastery in Paris in the seventeenth century, entered into this rest and learned to practice the presence of God. Once, when he was very ill, he was asked whether he would like to live a little longer in order that he might still grow in holiness, or die and enter into the blessedness of the saints. He replied that he left the choice with God, for he wished only to await God's will in peace. John Wesley also records a number of such cases in his journal. In this rest all is done for the love of God; the strident call of duty, the imperative voice of law, or the motive of personal pleasure no longer are the governing factors in the life. Fear of the wrath of God as an incentive to keep His commandments has gone forever, for perfect love has come in and has cast out such fear (1 John 4:18). Is the task distasteful to the flesh? Then the disciple is glad to do it with a willing heart out of love for his Master, for he "serves the Lord Christ" (Colossians 3:24), and of Him he will receive the "recompense of reward" (Hebrews 10:35). Is the work so very small? Still all is well, for ***the Lord looks not at the size of the work, but at***

the willing love of the one who does it. Does He need our service? Can He not, at a word, speak a world into existence, or raise up from stones children to Abraham? Is the work too great? Love never fails; and He who has chosen the task will prove by many a sign and wonder that He will be with him unto the end whom He has chosen to perform the work.

All things are possible to him
That can in Jesu's name believe.
Lord, I no more Thy truth blaspheme,
Thy truth I lovingly receive;
I can, I do believe in Thee,
All things are possible to me.[7]

—Charles Wesley—

"Consider the Lilies of the Field..."

And why take ye thought for raiment? Consider the lilies of the field, how they grow; they toil not, neither do they spin: [29]And yet I say unto you, That even Solomon in all his glory was not arrayed like one of these.

Matthew 6:28-29

Let us consider the lilies. There has been a concern among the commentators, who wish to rightly expound the truth of the Scriptures, as to what those lilies were that the Lord Jesus was speaking about. Was it the *lilium candidum*, a fair white lily that grows in Syria, although not in a wild state? Was it the lotus, or the anemone, or the tulip? Was the color scarlet, violet, or orange? All these varieties and colors have had their supporters; but does not the Lord say *lilies*? He is emphasizing that one kind of lily is not sufficient to describe the quality, the beauty, the character of one of His saints. Does He not say that "the righteous shall flourish like the palm tree: he shall grow like a cedar in Lebanon" (Psalm 92:12)? Neither the upright, resilient, and fruitful palm, nor the sturdy, fragrant, disease-resisting cedar can alone typify one of His children; both are needed to give an adequate image. So put all the virtues of many forms of flowers with all the glories of their diverse coloring together if you would describe the exceeding fairness of the Bride, the Lamb's wife. He gave Himself that she might be sanctified and cleansed —"a glorious church, not having spot or wrinkle, or any such thing; but that it should be holy and without blemish" (Ephesians 5:26,27).

"...They Toil Not..."

These lilies toil not. They have entered (as we have seen) into the rest that remains for the people of God. There is no perspiring anxiety to work for God; no passionate or sentimental human appeal is needed to touch their hearts, for they are moved with the compassionate love of Jesus. Like the early Christians, they have not to be constantly reminded to witness for the Lord Jesus (there are no exhortations to do this or emotional appeals for funds to carry out this work in the epistles), for the Holy Spirit has come and, having come, He ever witnesses through them to the Lord Jesus.

"...Neither Do They Spin..."

These lilies spin not. They no longer attempt to spin and weave and cut out and make up their own garments of righteousness, for they have learned that they have received "forgiveness of sins and inheritance amongst those who are sanctified by faith" that is in Jesus (Acts 26:18). They have a love gift given to them—the gift of their Lord's seamless dress which comes on them from above; it cannot be put on in any other way. The kings and priests of Christ's kingdom, then, do not spin; their garments are made for them of fine linen, a love gift of holiness through faith in Jesus. They are not garments of their own, manufactured through suppression of sin, and self-righteousness; for as Ezekiel says, "They shall not gird themselves with anything that causeth sweat" (Ezekiel 44:18). "Let us be glad and rejoice and give honour to Him: for the marriage of the Lamb is come, and His wife hath made herself ready. And to her was granted that she should be arrayed in fine linen, clean and white: for the fine linen is the righteousness of saints" (Revelation 19:7,8).

Holiness by faith in Jesus,
Not by effort of thine own,
Sin's dominion crushed and broken
By the power of grace alone,
God's own holiness within thee,
His own beauty on thy brow;
This shall be thy pilgrim brightness,
This thy blessèd portion now.[8]

—Frances Ridley Havergal—

"...Even Solomon in All His Glory..."

The adorning of the lily has a different quality than that of man. Solomon's regal robes were most carefully preserved, and used only for state occasions. They were held in most special honor, for, arrayed in his robes, Solomon looked a king indeed; without them, he looked like any other man. No one was allowed to wear purple in the days of imperial Rome but the emperor only. Until almost recent history, the dress of the different classes of society was, by tradition and also by law (in Europe), assigned to them. There was severe punishment for those who presumed to dress above their station in life. Why was this? Because, as in the days of Solomon, without extraordinary dress, folk appeared to be just ordinary people. I regret to have to remind you that in the days of the apostles there was no such thing as clerical attire; they had no need to dress to look different, because they were different. As ecclesiastical formalism grew, the anointing of the Holy Spirit no longer rested upon the presbyters, the ministers of the Church, and they did what the world around them did—they wore special religious vestments—some dressing like the priests of the Old Covenant, the ministry of which has passed away. It is not that it is wrong to wear special clerical robes; it is just unnecessary where the pastor and his flock are under the anointing of the Holy Spirit.

"...Was Not Arrayed Like One of These."

The Lord Jesus has a different viewpoint from man; in His eyes His lilies have a glory far beyond the most majestic king—even Solomon. But their array can be trampled upon; the flower can be bruised and the beauty dimmed. But, patience! For below the surface of things, deep down, is the true lily, and from its *corm*[9] and roots will come up again another flower as fair and as glorious as the first. As Elizabeth Barrett Browning says:

Very whitely still
The lilies of our lives may reassure
Their blossoms from their roots, accessible
Alone to heavenly dews.[10]

Man does not recognize the glory of the saints of God; they have a different quality, hidden from natural eyes, away underneath. Their adornment is "the hidden man of the heart, in that which is not corruptible," even "the ornament of a meek and quiet spirit, which in the sight of God is of great price" (1 Peter 3:4). This is something that the best religion cannot create. We can make a fair imitation, and today the plastic or silk imitation lilies which are manufactured would deceive a florist—at a distance—but they are not alive, and they cannot grow. It is food for thought that some churches have these imitation lilies on their altars; I wonder if that is a parable? Only the Holy Spirit, "the Lord and Giver of life," can produce Christ's lilies.

So lilies grow in rest, without constant effort, and in doing so are clothed with garments of glory and beauty. But, although they grow so fair, so straight and tall, yet their feet are in the earth. This deserves a comment. All the King's lilies must remember that although their heads and hearts are in heaven, their feet are on the earth. They are *in* the world, but not *of* it. One whose head, heart, and feet are all on earth ceases to be His lily at all; and one whose feet, heart, and head are all in the heavenlies tends to become a fanatic. Feet on earth keep the heart and head lowly so that the child of God can walk in a true faith and grow in it.

Where Lilies Grow

We have spoken of the "how," but let us now consider the *where* of lily growth. "As the lily among thorns, so is my love among the daughters" (Song of Songs 2:2). Lilies often have to grow among the thorns. The Lord often places one of His most precious saints in the roughest circumstances and amongst the wicked, who are as thorns. Very bitter, petty, carping, and sarcastic are the world's children, and they know well how to wound the sensitive spirit of a child of God. The Lord, whose head was crowned with thorns, has fullest sympathy because of His knowledge and experience, and will comfort the one who rests by faith in Him. The water-lily, as Tennyson says, knows how to take refuge from the chilly darkness and buffeting winds of the night by folding up her flowers and sinking beneath the surface. Let us apply the poet's words and do the same by finding our refuge in Jesus.

Now folds the lily all her sweetness up,
And slips into the bosom of the lake;
So fold thyself, My dearest, thou and slip
Into My bosom, and be lost in Me.[11]

A lily among thorns, or a lily growing from the mud, is all the more lovely by contrast. The superscription[12] of Psalm 45 says that it is a "Song of loves upon Shoshannim." ***Shoshannim*** means ***lilies***. It is a lily psalm—a song of loves concerning the Lord and His lilies. He says that if we (like Ruth) will forget our own people and our father's house (verse 10), that is, if we will go out after Him, leaving all and following, then the King will greatly desire our beauty. We shall be "all glorious within," having a pure heart, and like the lilies whose dress was more glorious than Solomon's, our clothing shall be of wrought gold (verse 13).

It will be thought by some that the nature we have been describing, which is the nature of Jesus and of His bride, will be weak, irresolute, and characterless. It is not so; those who have grown like the lily have proved strong in faith and patience, and the names of many are emblazoned forever on the martyr rolls of Heaven. When Solomon built his magnificent temple—a faint type of the more glorious one built of living stones, to be a habitation of the Most High God—he had two bronze pillars cast to represent the strength of the place. One of the pillars he called "Jachin" and the other "Boaz." *Jachin* means *He [God] will establish; Boaz* means *In Him [God] is strength.* "Upon the top of the pillars was lily work" (1 Kings 7:13-22). This is the Lord's picture of His saints (and especially of the elders of the Church), men and women with strength of character, through whom He establishes the Church, but who are adorned with the lily character of Jesus.

The Lord and His Lilies

I am not one of those whom the Lord honors with visions, but I thank God for all those like Joseph and Daniel who dream dreams, and for all the Pauls and Johns who see visions, under the glory of the New Covenant, as Joel promised.[13] Once during a time of waiting upon God in the company of two other pastors (who were men of experience in the things of the Spirit), a vision was given to us.

In that vision, the Lord Jesus Christ was seen walking along the road—in His arms a number of lilies; but each one was broken, and He was weeping. With many tears He took each broken lily and sadly dropped it onto the road. It was revealed to us that these were the backsliders who had gone back to a life of sin and who had refused, despite His pleading, to return to Him. Then again the Lord was seen walking down the road, once more with lilies in His hands. But these had crushed stems and were useless. He was brokenhearted and, with tears, He regretfully dropped them on the road too, for these were those whom He had sought to perfect by chastening. However, instead of being exercised thereby,[14] they had turned away from Him and had gone for comfort back into the pleasures of the world. Yet again we saw Him, walking with a radiant countenance through a field of growing, sweet-scented and upright white lilies. As He walked among them, He laughed for joy and caressed them with His fingers, for these were His children who had asked for grace that they might kiss His rod, lean upon His staff, and ever increase in their love for Him.

> *"Behold I come quickly; hold that fast which thou hast, that no man take thy crown. Him that overcometh will I make a pillar in the temple of my God and he shall go no more out: and I will write upon him the name of my God... and My new name."*
>
> *Revelation 3:11,12*

Endnotes for Chapter 6

---

1. *Tophet*, mentioned in Isaiah 30:33, was a place of burning in the Valley of Hinnom (*Ge hinnom*, from which the word *Gehenna*, translated *Hell*, is derived) outside of Jerusalem, and, as such, is a type of Hell.

2. *Chamois* (pronounced "*sham*-mee"): a sort of goat-antelope native to the mountainous regions of Europe and parts of Asia

3. *Theophany*—an appearance of God in human form to a person

4. These are the full lyrics, but they are also included on page 191 in the appendix.

5. *Imago:* an insect in its final, adult, sexually mature, and (typically) winged state

6. While Jesus' narration (note that He did not call this a parable) names the poor beggar as *Lazarus*, He never names the rich man. However, tradition has bestowed upon this rich man the name of Dives (DI-veez). The name is actually nothing more than the transliteration of the word "rich"—*dives*—in the Vulgate (Latin) translation of Luke 16:19 ("*homo quidam erat dives...*").

7. From the hymn ***All Things Are Possible to Him***. As will be seen from the full lyrics on page 192, this song is a declaration of the God-given faith to receive a pure heart.

8. Quoted from Havergal's hymn ***Church of God, Beloved and Chosen***, which is found on page 193.

9. *Corm:* the enlarged, fleshy, underground part of the stem, similar to a bulb

10. This quote comes from Elizabeth Barrett Browning's work, "Sonnets from the Portuguese," Canto XXIV, from the book entitled simply *Poems.*

11. As indicated, this is from one of Alfred, Lord Tennyson's poems, "Now Sleeps the Crimson Petal," from the book *The Princess*.

12. Many psalms have a *superscription* (a "verse zero," if you will), which can indicate the psalm's author, the inspiration for its writing, or the tune to which it was to be played. For example, in Psalm 45, the psalm under consideration, the superscription reads as follows:

To the chief Musician
upon Shoshannim,
for the sons of Korah,
Maschil,
A Song of loves.

The superscriptions are considered part of the inspired text, not to be confused with "helpful" (but non-inspired and arbitrary) psalm headings provided in some translations.

13. See Joel 2:28-29.

14. The allusion is to Hebrews 12:11.

·7·
The Preparation of the Man of Faith

GOD IS PREPARING MEN OF FAITH to do great deeds before this age closes. We have not yet seen the perfect fulfillment of the Lord's Word when He said, *"Verily, verily, I say unto you, He that believeth on Me, the works that I do shall he do also, and greater works than these shall he do; because I go unto My Father"* (John 14:12). Many have asked the question: "When were these words fulfilled?" and there has been much kneading and pulling the Scriptures into shape in an attempt to answer it. When the full time has come, the truth of His words will be completely demonstrated. Even now, He is preparing men and women for that time, to walk with Him in faith.

My honest readers will confess with me that they do not like to be brought into those troublesome and harsh circumstances where a triumphant faith is necessary. We naturally prefer the teaching that if one pays one's tithes to the Lord and also gives a bit extra occasionally, then the Lord will bless us with physical, temporal, and spiritual prosperity. This is a nice, comfortable, *Western* doctrine that seems to operate and fit in well with the sunny skies of California; but it is most out of place in a Communist prison camp under the cutting, icy winds of bleak, atheistic Siberia, where it does not work at all. For any doctrine to be true, it must be *universally* true. Of course, we all like smooth things. When David was faced with troubles and trials he said, *"O that I had wings like a dove! for then would I fly away and be at rest.... I would hasten my escape from the windy storm and tempest"* (Psalm 55:6,8). He wrote this Psalm when he was fleeing from Absalom, and he calls it a *Maschil*—that is, a psalm of *instruction* for those under similar circumstances, as was, for example, the Lord Jesus when He was betrayed by Judas.

The Most High says, "If ye will not believe, surely ye shall not be established" (Isaiah 7:9). This word is given so that we should know that we are only established and made pillars in the temple of God by a living faith; but we cannot live by faith unless there is in our lives a need to exercise it.

Preparation in Canaan

Have you left the land of Egypt for Canaan? That is, have you left the worldliness of this world for the place of living in obedience to the indwelling Holy Spirit? Then notice the marked difference between the two spiritual countries:

> *For the land, whither thou goest in to possess it, is not as the land of Egypt, from whence ye came out, where thou sowest thy seed, and wateredst it with thy foot, as a garden of herbs. [11]But the land, whither ye go to possess it, is a land of hills and valleys, and drinketh water of the rain of heaven.*
>
> *Deuteronomy 11:10-11*

In other words, Egypt was a place of social security and materialism, where, by constitutional theory at least, there was no lack. You took what water you wanted from the Nile and ran it into an irrigation channel. By breaking down temporarily the mud sides of the little waterway with your foot, you gave the land as much water as it needed, and then made up with your foot again the breach in the low mud wall. There was no reason why Egypt should not always prosper and be rich; and so it was, for some. But it was the land of deepest misery for others.

Did they ever think that it all depended upon the depth of flow in the Nile, and that it was God's Nile?

What of Canaan? No Nile was there. Jordan did not irrigate Palestine. All depended upon the clouds of Heaven. Unless the rains came, there was drought and starvation; it was a land of faith, where the farmer had to trust in God. It was a land where men of faith could be produced. God trained no men of faith in Egypt. The Old Testament contains many a record of how God prepared His men and women of faith in the land of Canaan. The epistle to the Hebrews says that time would fail in an attempt to tell of all those who under the Old Covenant obtained a good report through faith. Hebrews chapter 11 contains a very incomplete list of the faith heroes of God. Let us also remember and take warning that not all those whom the Lord put upon trial came through.

Signs Are Not a Sign of Faith

There came a time when Hezekiah was sick unto death (2 Kings 20). His time had come. In the infallible judgment of the Lord, he was now to go to Abraham's bosom; but he wept and mourned and sulkily turned his face to the wall. He did not accept, by faith, that the Lord knew best; but God *did* know best. The Lord graciously (but reluctantly) granted him an extension of fifteen years, and again Hezekiah's weakness of faith was revealed. He said, "What shall be the sign that the LORD will heal me?" (2 Kings 20:8) Faith never asks for a sign, because it believes the Word of the Lord; it is weak faith, faith tinctured with doubting, which asks for a sign. If you are a sign seeker, you must be delivered from this weakness before you can become a man of faith. It is popular in the so-called "Charismatic" circles to look for signs. A very familiar saying is, "I wanted to test the matter, to see if it was the Lord's will; so I put out a fleece, as did Gideon" (Judges 6:36-40). A statement such as this is a clear indication that first, this one does not know the Lord's will; and second, he has a doubting mind.

If the Lord has spoken to you, then do what the Lord has said. If the Lord has not spoken, then wait upon Him until He does. Hezekiah, like Gideon, asked for a sign because he doubted, not because he believed. If Hezekiah had been a believer with his whole heart and had accepted the Lord's word in the first case, he would not have lived to produce a son, Manasseh, who became a byword for wickedness in Israel, and he would not have shown the treasures of Israel to the Babylonians, thereby inciting their cupidity and eventual possession of those treasures.

Conversely, Abraham is the Lord's example of faith. He asked for no sign, but did what the Lord commanded and believed for the impossible. Therefore, the Lord gave him signs and made him the father of all those who believe. It is written in the Scriptures, for our instruction, that the apostles "went forth and preached everywhere, the Lord working with them, and confirming the word with signs following" (Mark 16:20). The signs did not come first and then, because of them, the apostles followed with the word of the Gospel; rather, they gave out that which the Lord put into their lips, and He confirmed His own Word with signs, proving the truth of their divinely inspired word. This order has been reversed nowadays; folks are taught to look for a sign and then they believe. This is, unhappily, particularly true in the modern teaching concerning the receiving of the Holy Spirit, so that in reality what these folk are believing for is a *sign*, and *not* the promise of the Father, which is the gift of the Holy Spirit to all those who repent and believe on the Lord Jesus Christ for salvation. The result is unstable, immature, emotion-controlled, doubting believers.

All signs are fallible, because they can be imitated or misunderstood; but the Word of the Lord alone is infallible, and is known as such to the one who receives it. The Spirit still speaks "expressly" (1 Timothy 4:1), which means "stated definitely, with clarity, not merely implied"; so that "My sheep hear My voice, and I know them, and they follow Me" (John 10:27).

Preparation in Weakness

A major part of the preparation of the man of faith is the work of the Holy Spirit in the crucifixion of self before service. One of our modern beliefs is that the Lord uses our strongest faculty as the spearhead behind which He concentrates His strength. This is an error. He uses ***weakness***—not strength—because only when we are in weakness have we no confidence in the flesh, so that our trust has to be wholly in Him. This is a truth that every man or woman of faith has to discover. The Lord will repeat the lesson again and again (for He is the God of patience) until this has been learned. When will the Church *believe*, not just recite, that "He hangs the earth upon nothing" (Job 26:7)? God's men of faith "out of weakness were made strong" (Hebrews 11:34). The Lord Jesus said to Paul, "My grace is sufficient for thee: for My strength is made perfect in weakness." Then says Paul, "Most gladly therefore will I rather glory in my infirmities, that the power of Christ may rest upon me" (2 Corinthians 12:9).

The strength of the Lord's spiritual leaders, who were to be examples to those following after, was made weakness before He made them His instruments. Let's look at some of these men.

Jacob

Consider Jacob, a man of much journeying, a self-made, self-reliant, capable man, and a pilgrim—as he emphasized to Pharaoh (Genesis 47:9). On Peniel God took away his greatest strength, his ability to walk and work, touching him in the muscle of his thigh so that all the rest of his days he limped—"he halted on his thigh" (Genesis 32:25, 31-32). Then and only then could his name be changed, because his nature had been changed, and he became "Israel"—"for as a prince hast thou power with God and with men, and hast prevailed" (Genesis 32:28). His strength was gone and all he could do was to cling. By His grace, the Lord strengthened him to hold on and so be blessed.

Contented now upon my thigh
I halt, till life's short journey end;
All helplessness, all weakness, I
On Thee alone for strength depend;
Nor have I power from Thee to move:
Thy nature and Thy name is Love.

Lame as I am, I take the prey,
Hell, earth, and sin with ease o'ercome;
I leap for joy, pursue my way,
And as a bounding hart fly home,
Through all eternity to prove
Thy nature and Thy name is Love.[1]

—Charles Wesley—

Most happy will those be who have a new name given to them in Heaven. "I will give him a white stone, and in the stone a new name written" (Revelation 2:17). All those who are named by God have a name that describes their character. In other days, names were significant, for a name imprinted upon any vessel would always describe the contents. So children, having been received as gifts from God, were by righteous parents offered back to Him that He might name and bless them. God has not changed; the Christian father, baptized in the Holy Spirit, may still name his children by the revelation of God, and it will be found that the names have prophetic significance. Let the world name their children after heathen deities or film stars, but let the people of God revert to Bible practice and seek a name from God. The Lord will give a name to all of His children in Heaven, according to their character. We shall have the name that we are—one that perfectly describes the person that we have allowed Him to make us. But, in addition, those who overcome will have given to them a new name that "no man knoweth saving he that receiveth it" (Revelation 2:17), a secret name of love used by the Lord only to them.

Moses

Where did Moses' strength lie? In his right hand! With this he had killed the Egyptian; with this he had defended the daughters of Jethro; and this was the hand that the Lord caused to become leprous. "Put now thy hand into thy bosom—behold, his hand was leprous as snow!" (Exodus 4:6) Could it have been made more contemptuous or weak? *Now* this hand could become, by God's enduement, the cleansed hand of power, to hold the rod, bring the plagues, divide the sea and smite the rock.

Isaiah

Where was Isaiah's power to be? In his lips! He was to be the great prophet of the Old Testament, the one who, more than any other, was to reveal Messiah. His lips had to be made weak, and as nothing, before God. Therefore he was given a vision of the Lord, high and lifted up, and at once he was convicted of having unclean lips. "Then said I, Woe is me! for I am undone ["dumb" in the original] because I am a man of unclean lips.... Then flew one of the *seraphim* unto me, having a live coal in his hand which he had taken with the tongs from off the altar, and he laid it upon my mouth and said, 'Lo, this has touched thy lips, and thine iniquity is taken away, and thy sin purged' " (Isaiah 6:5-7). After that the Lord could say, "Go and tell this people," to a completely willing Isaiah.

Peter

What was the chief characteristic of Peter? His impulse! His energy! His action! This had to be brought to the cross so that Peter's spring of action would not be in his flesh, but would come from the indwelling Spirit of God. The Lord dealt with Peter at His own betrayal; for, out of love, Peter had followed Jesus to the High Priest's palace, and it was there that all Peter's strength was turned into weakness. After this, the Lord could use Peter's pioneering spirit to unlock the door of Pentecost, first to the Jews at Jerusalem and later to the Gentiles at Caesarea.

Paul

Saul of Tarsus was mastered by his intelligence. It was his dominating characteristic, his outstanding feature. His clear-thinking mind saw things in sharp focus; yet he was wrong. His spiritual blindness caused him to spend his days injuring the God he professed and wished to serve. This great strength had to be turned into weakness. A heavenly laser beam from the glorious countenance of the risen Son struck him in the head, and he fell to the earth, weak, yielded, blind, and having now no power, not even to direct his own steps. Someone led him by the hand and brought him into Damascus. There, a lowly follower of the once despised Nazarene laid his hands upon Saul so that he received his sight and was filled with the Holy Spirit (Acts

9:1-20). From that point on, Saul had no confidence in the flesh, so God could use his mind to write those wonderful epistles. Saul, son of Adam, and of Benjamin, became known as Paul ("little"), son of God. This was the man who, his intelligence being renewed and energized by the Spirit, was used of God to be the wise master builder of the churches.

John the Baptist

We must give special consideration to John the Baptist. He is, *par excellence*, the type of man whom the Lord will use to herald His coming. For just as John was the chosen one to proclaim that the Kingdom of Heaven was at hand (that is, had drawn nigh), so there will be those who with an authority and power greater than John's shall declare that the manifestation of the Kingdom "is near, even at the door." Are the men and women of faith, then, to be greater than John? *Yes*, for that is the Lord's will and provision. John was "filled with the Holy Spirit from his mother's womb" (Luke 1:15); but the "Holy Spirit was not yet given because that Jesus was not yet glorified" (John 7:39). There was to be a giving of the Spirit, because of Christ's death and resurrection, under the New Covenant, far beyond the receiving of the Spirit under the Old. Jesus said, "Verily, I say unto you, among them that are born of women there hath not risen a greater than John the Baptist: notwithstanding, he that is least in the kingdom of Heaven is greater than he" (Matthew 11:11). How can this be? Because John was born of woman, of the line of Adam, a great *servant* of the Living God, anointed with power by the Holy Spirit, to fulfill his service; but those who are of the Kingdom of Heaven have been "born again" not of flesh, but of the Spirit of God, and by His great adoption are sons of the Most High. Thus does the New Covenant far outshine the Old Covenant. "John did no miracle" (John 10:41), but the Lord Jesus said of those who no longer were to be called "servants" by Him (John 15:15) that greater things than even He had done were to be done by them, because He was going to the glory of His Father (John 14:12), and from that place of power He would direct the affairs of the Church.

Preparation of the Bride by Men of Faith

Before any special manifestation of God, one is sent by Him as a herald to prepare the way. This is a divine principle, that there should always be the "voice of him that crieth in the wilderness, 'Prepare ye the way of the Lord,' " before He comes. The last of the Old Testament prophets proclaimed, "Behold, I will send you Elijah the prophet before the coming of the great and dreadful day of the LORD" (Malachi 4:5). This does not mean the personal return of Elijah, but one coming in the same Spirit and power as Elijah. John was not Elijah, but the Lord Jesus said of John, "And if ye will receive it, this is Elijah which was for to come" (Matthew 11:14). John did not completely fulfill the prophecy of Isaiah. Isaiah said that subsequent to the voice of him who cried in the wilderness, crooked things would be made straight, and rough places plain, and "the glory of the LORD shall be revealed and all flesh shall see it together" (Isaiah 40:3-5). This has not yet taken place. Before the second coming of the Lord in His glory and majesty, there will be other Johns, other Elijahs; not just one, but many, all over the earth, who will proclaim under the full anointing of the Spirit the immediate appearing and triumph of the Christ. John, in the same spirit as Elijah, appeared in the land of Israel only, for that was where Messiah at His first coming was soon to be revealed. But at the second coming of the Lord Jesus Christ, He is not to be seen only in Palestine, for "every eye shall see Him" (Revelation 1:7). So there must be a universal testimony heralding His universal appearing. **Before the Lord comes *for* His people, He will come *to* His people**, for they must be prepared as a bride adorned for her husband" (Revelation 21:2). This coming to His people will be a visitation of the Holy Spirit—a time of great revival, with a special emphasis upon personal holiness, accompanied by extraordinary acts of power, as every revival has been since Pentecost. Revival is the Lord visiting His people (and through them, others) in grace. When He visits a people in wrath, as at Sodom, it is judgment. Before every visitation in judgment, He first visits in mercy, for "mercy rejoiceth against judgment" (James 2:13).

Preparation in Obscurity: Locusts & Wild Honey

God prepares His men of faith in secret places. Like John the Baptist, they are hidden in the desert until the time of their showing. They still dwell outside of the camp, and are left there by the religious authorities after their revealing, as were John the Baptist, Martin Luther, John Wesley, William Booth, and a thousand others. But some time after their decease, their followers are received back again, when they fit more easily into the religious scene because the anointing of the Spirit has gone. "In the desert" does not mean that they are ascetics, but that they are hidden, despised, unknown, and unwanted. Joseph was hidden in the pit and the dungeons; Moses was for forty years in the back of the desert; Paul went into Arabia, where lies one of the greatest deserts in the world. Jesus, after He received the Spirit, spent forty days in the wilderness.

What of the food of these heralds of the Lord? It is not manna, but locusts and wild honey (Matthew 3:4; Mark 1:6). "Locusts" does not mean the fruit of the carob tree as some have supposed, but rather the locust insect which was permitted to the Israelites as clean food (Leviticus 11:22). This forms a sufficiently nourishing, but very monotonous, diet. The honey was collected at the risk of stings—wild bee stings, sharper and more potent than those of the hive bee. Honey is sweet, but there could be a most unpleasant side to the sweetness. The joys of the man of God are likely to be blended with pain. Yet honey means flowers; there are flowers of comfort. Locusts are the most devouring force on earth; they will turn a garden of Eden into a barren wilderness. The very things that seem to eat life away—problems, trials, losses, misunderstandings—are the diet to nourish God's man in hiding, who all unknowingly is awaiting his ministry in the revival that will herald the Lord's coming again. There will be nothing about him to entice, neither form nor manner nor figure nor dress; rather he will be dressed like John in a raiment of the commonest cloth. John's was woven of camel's hair. That means the man of God will not be among the elite who wear soft raiment and who charm by their elegance.

What do you say to these things? Some will say with me, "Beloved Lord, despite the fact that I am what I am, loving ease, disliking reproof and chastening, please make me the one You want me to be, by the exercise of Your grace. Here is my heart. Here is my will. Take them, and make me to will and to do Your good pleasure. Amen!" Then:

His purposes will ripen fast,
Unfolding every hour;
The bud may have a bitter taste,
But sweet will be the flower.[2]

—William Cowper—

---

1. ***Wrestling Jacob*** (also called by its first line, *Come, O Thou Traveller Unknown*) was one of Pastor Gutteridge's favorite hymns. The unabridged lyrics are found in on page 195 in the appendix.

2. Pastor Gutteridge ends by quoting Cowper's (pronounced "Cooper") famous work, ***God Moves in a Mysterious Way,*** also found in the appendix on page 198.

·8·
The Certainties of Faith

TRUE FAITH ALWAYS RESULTS IN CERTAINTY. How wonderful to be certain in an uncertain world! Faith always homes in on the target; there are no near misses; there is no such thing as experimentation, because faith knows, like its Author, "the end from the beginning." The men of faith walk with confidence, they keep their equilibrium, they press towards the mark, they are like the cherubim who have feet that are "straight feet... they went every one straight forward, whither the Spirit was to go, they went, and they turned not when they went" (Ezekiel 1:12).

The Certainty of Action, Reaction, and Counteraction

There are great underlying spiritual laws that like ocean tides govern and affect the affairs of earth and men. Too often we forget that we are the battleground for the warfare, waged on a titanic scale, between good and evil. It is seen in the Garden of Eden, where the evil one, seeking to undo what God had done, commenced his defiling and destroying work on earth. It was recommenced after the Flood, being exemplified by the unclean raven and the pure dove going out, each on its mission over the earth. It was climaxed at Calvary when the everlasting victory over evil was won and sentence pronounced. The execution of the sentence was delayed, but now is drawing to its fulfillment—in our day. So we experience hopes and fears, ups and downs, crests and troughs, hills and valleys, peace and war, and shall continue to do so until the end of the way. One of these great cosmic tides, with its inevitable ebb and flow, is the universal experience of Action, Reaction, and Counteraction.

The Almighty God commences an action; the evil one always opposes with a reaction; God then brings in a counteraction. There are many illustrations of this. We will look at a few examples; however, having been introduced to this principle, you will discern many others for yourself.

The Almighty One by His commanding Word brought into existence all creation: that is action. There followed reaction, when the devil caused the Fall. Then came the great counteraction, when God promised the coming of the Messiah. The evil one always seems to have frustrated the purpose of God; but each time the Most High uses it to bring in a far higher and greater blessing than the one that has been lost. Learn this, wise reader; the knowledge will prove invaluable to you. When the Lord blesses you, hold on for the reaction and, when it comes, do not despair; it has been permitted to lift you up to a greater glory.

More Examples

Here are other examples. Action—God sent His Son. Reaction—Satan caused Him to be put to death. Counteraction—God raised Him from the dead and gave Him a name above every name, so that in the name of Jesus every knee shall bow. The Lord is going to act soon, in sending the last and greatest showers of the Latter Rain in revival. The evil one will react by causing great tribulation, distress, wars, and pestilences; but the great counteraction will be the second coming of the Lord Jesus

Christ. After that will come one of the most blessed actions of God, the millennium of peace, when through the righteous reigning of Jesus and His glorified saints the earth shall be full of the knowledge of the Lord as the waters cover the sea. The evil one will be bound for this period and confined away from the earth in the bottomless pit (Revelation 20:3). Because of his imprisonment, during that blessed time there will be no need for that word of Peter, so necessary now: "Be sober, be vigilant, for your adversary the devil, as a roaring lion walketh about, seeking whom he may devour" (1 Peter 5:8). When he is let out, there will be a great reaction, and the nations will once more be deceived. Led by the devil, they will insurrect against the Lord and compass the camp of the saints about (Revelation 20:7-9). Then comes the great and final and everlasting counteraction—the complete and utter destruction of evil, the eternal imprisonment of the evil one, the final judgment, and new heavens and a new earth with "no more death, neither sorrow nor crying, neither... any more pain," and God making "all things new" (Revelation 21:4,5). When God makes all things new, there will come new great tides of everlasting action, with reaction and God's necessary counteraction gone forever.

Let us consider again this great principle, so that by the repetition of the lesson this great certainty of faith may be one of your most carefully preserved spiritual jewels. The great action of God in sending the Holy Spirit upon the small band of believing Jews at Pentecost (Acts 2) would of necessity precipitate a great reaction, because of the danger to the enemy's kingdom now that the Spirit of power had come. The reaction came. The Jewish hierarchy was used by the devil against the early church: the "priests and the captain of the temple and the Sadducees came upon them" (Acts 4:1); and the final result of the reaction was that the first martyr, Stephen, was put to death (Acts 7) for an example of what the church could expect in the future from the devil's wrath. Now see the Lord's most wonderful counteraction to this. First, He sent an angel and let the apostles out of jail (Acts 5:18-21). But, most wonderful of all, He converted the chief persecutor, Saul (Acts 9), and made him also an apostle of Jesus!

A Final Example

There are so many scriptural examples of this great truth that this book would run to an inordinate length if more were given. Still, we will consider one final example—one which followed immediately after Paul's conversion. God made an even more wonderful action than at the original Pentecost, when He sent the Holy Spirit upon Cornelius and his Gentile friends (Acts 10). The Jewish race was but a small one and their influence limited, but the Gentiles were the dominant people and had spread over all the earth. It needs no emphasis of mine to remind the reader that this outpouring of the Holy Spirit upon the Gentiles would stir up the malice of Satan even more. Until this time, the enemy had used as his instrument the deceived and angry Jews with their small measure of power and their limited armed forces, which they could use, by permission of the government, against their own countrymen only. Now Satan brings up to combat against the Spirit-anointed Gentiles his greatest weapon—the iron-willed, ruthless, and unconquerable Romans, figured by that beast of Daniel's visions, "diverse from all the others, exceeding dreadful, whose teeth were of iron, and his nails of brass, which devoured, brake in pieces, and stamped the residue with his feet" (Daniel 7:19). King Herod Agrippa at once killed James, the brother of John, with the sword. Peter also was condemned to death, put into prison, and watched over by a Roman guard (Acts 12:1-6). We can appreciate Peter's situation better by considering these points as background:

- When the body of Jesus was put into the tomb, it was a *Jewish* guard that watched over His body—a guard which could be bribed to tell the lie that the disciples stole the body away whilst they slept.[1]

- By contrast, if a Roman soldier slept on duty, he was executed. If a Roman soldier had accepted a bribe and had allowed his prisoner to escape, he was executed. If Roman soldiers allowed, *for any reason*, their prisoners to escape, they were executed. For instance, when Paul and Silas were imprisoned at Philippi and suddenly there was a great earthquake and every prisoner's bonds were loosed, the jailer would have killed himself, supposing that they had fled; but Paul cried with a loud voice, "Do thyself no harm, for we are all here" (Acts 16:27-28). Again, when Paul was a prisoner on his way to Rome on the Alexandrian corn ship (a regular sailing taking Egypt's corn to Rome for the supply of bread for the inhabitants), a batch of prisoners was on board with him under a Roman guard. When the ship struck on the rocks of Malta, the counsel of the soldiers was to kill the prisoners. This was in order to save their own lives, for if any prisoner escaped, their lives would have been forfeited; but the centurion kept them from their purpose (Acts 27:42-43).

We have then, in this Gentile Pentecost, an entirely different reaction, for Satan brought in the most powerful force on earth to sustain his kingdom. From a human point of view, deliverance was impossible. Peter was committed to the keeping of four quaternions of soldiers. (The word in the Greek original is *tetradion*, a Roman military term, meaning *a squad of four.*) Peter was kept helpless, chained between two soldiers, while two others of the four kept watch outside the door of the cell. This watch was changed every three hours. Apart from this, there was a second guarding or ward that had to be passed before the courtyard was entered; this had great iron gates leading out into the city. Now see what comfort and peace surrounds the man of faith. See the certainty of Peter's faith, which enables him to sleep under these impossible conditions. The Lord Jesus had once told him (John 21:18) that when he was old and blind he would be led to a martyr's death, glorifying God. Peter was to be executed on the morrow; but he slept! Why? Just because he believed God! He was certain that he would not die—how could he?—when he was yet neither old, nor blind, and was able to gird himself! So Peter rested—the rest of faith. Then the Lord came in with a mighty counteraction: an angel put the guards to sleep, awoke Peter, dissolved his chains, opened the prison doors, and led Peter out a free man through the gates into the city (Acts 12:7-11).

Notice, please—and let this be a check to fanaticism—that Peter had to do the things that he *could* do, and then the angel did the things that he *could not* do. Peter could put his own cloak on, bind his girdle around himself, and put his own sandals on his feet. The angel could have done these things, but would not. Peter could not send the soldiers to sleep, loose his chains, or open the prison doors, so the angel did what Peter could not do. Fanaticism would have expected the angel to do everything, with the result that the angel would have done nothing. It is faith—balanced! pure! certain!—that sees God work miracles.

When the Lord raised Lazarus from the dead (John 11:38-44), He first commanded the men to remove the round stone door from the front of the tomb. He could have rolled it away at a word, but what the men *could* do, they *must* do. Then He did what they could not do: He called Lazarus alive out of the tomb. When the women came to the tomb of Jesus (Mark 16:1-4) bringing more spices to preserve His body, they were anxious, asking, "Who will roll the stone away for us?"—for the stone was very great. But because they could not do it, and it was necessary in God's providence that it should be done, an angel was sent who rolled the stone away at a touch. Is the work of faith clear to you now? You must do what you *can* do, and then the Lord will do what you *cannot* do. The great need of the man of faith is mental and spiritual balance.

Greatest of all in God's great counteraction—greater than Peter's deliverance, greater than confounding the devil's attempt, in his reaction, to crush the infant Church through his great iron monster, the Roman beast—was that the Holy Spirit spoke to the Church saying, "Separate for me Barnabas and Saul for the work whereunto I have called them" (Acts 13:1-4). What was the work? To take the gospel to the *Gentiles* throughout the whole world, and particularly to the Roman Empire. Through this divine calling, we Gentiles have come into the faith.

The Certainty of God's Promise: *Whosoever* and *Whatsoever*

The Author of faith speaks and acts with complete certainty and utmost authority. It is His will that His children of faith should, in their measure, speak and act with a like certainty and authority. When He called the young Samuel to be His prophet, He first proved his faith by testing his obedience, and then the Lord "let none of his words fall to the ground" (1 Samuel 3:19). In other words, what Samuel said would happen *did* happen; God brought it to pass. If the Lord did this for one of His great servants under the Old Covenant, how much more will He do it for His sons under the New Covenant? This is what the Lord Jesus confirmed when He said to His disciples:

> ***Whosoever****... shall not doubt in his heart, but shall believe that those things which he saith shall come to pass; he shall have* ***whatsoever*** *he saith.*
>
> *Mark 11:23*

Here are two clear, unequivocal words, carefully chosen by the Lord who is the Logos, the Word. It is impossible for Him to lie. ***Whosoever*** means "anyone, without exception," who does not doubt in his heart. ***Whatsoever*** means "anything, without exception." Then, seeing that there is this amazing promise, why is there not more work done for God? Why? Why not more prayers answered? Why not more miracles of faith performed? Why not more backsliders restored? Why? We could ask a thousand like questions! **It is because the *certainties* of faith are only for those who will fulfill the *conditions* of faith.** We have devoted a chapter to the conditions of faith,[2] but the time has come in your patient progress through this book when the subject must be considered more deeply.

Who Qualifies as "Whosoever"?

The promise of "whosoever" is open to any believing child of the Father *who will abide in the Son, through the grace and power of the indwelling Holy Spirit.* This promise is for the sons and daughters of the Most High. It is for those who have been consciously brought into new birth by the Holy Spirit and who have the inevitable witness thereto: "Because ye are sons, God hath sent forth the Spirit of His Son into your hearts, crying, 'Abba, Father' " (Galatians 4:6).

This witness of the Spirit is *not*, most certainly ***not***, our mental assent to a biblical statement of doctrine; it is an inward, conscious certainty, for "the Spirit Himself beareth witness with our spirit, that we are the children of God" (Romans 8:16). (However, God will withdraw even this if we attempt to make it a substitute for faith.) There is no question that the offer of eternal life is open to all the sons of Adam. "Whosoever will, let him take the water of life freely" (Revelation 22:17). Nevertheless, some have tried to put their humanly conceived, doctrinal limit upon the open, free, boundless mercy of the limitless God.

Only those who have received this gift of God and have become new creatures qualify for the truth of the "whosoever" in the great promise of Jesus. They may ask for whatsoever they will and receive it. The unsaved "whosoever" outside of the Kingdom may come in; and once he is in, he becomes part of the saved "whosoever" who may ask and believe for what he will, and receive it.

What Qualifies as "Whatsoever"?

Now let us consider the conditions of receiving the "whatsoever." The Lord Jesus unfolded these to His disciples when He spoke about Himself as being the True Vine (John 15):

> *If ye abide in Me and My words abide in you, ye shall ask what ye will and it shall be done unto you.*
>
> *John 15:7*

He further says,

> *I have chosen you and ordained you, that ye should go and bring forth fruit and that your fruit should remain; that **whatsoever** ye shall ask of the Father in My name, He may give it you.*
>
> *John 15:16*

He adds,

> *And in that day ye shall ask Me nothing. Verily, verily, I say unto you, **whatsoever** ye shall ask the Father in My name He will give it you.*
>
> *John 16:23*

The conditions are:

- that we are in the Vine;

- that we are abiding in Him;
- that we are producing fruit that remains, which means that we are mature, for only mature trees bring forth much fruit; and,
- that a time period is set—"In that day."

So experience in Christ is necessary, and experience is the result of patient, constant abiding in Him, although it is not the years of being a Christian that matter, but the depth and constancy of the abiding. "In that day" means the day of His resurrection—His triumphant return from the dead in victory—resulting in the day of the descent of the Spirit to indwell and empower His disciples. It is this present Gospel day.

The Reality of "In My Name"

There is a much misunderstood further condition: "Whatsoever ye shall ask the Father ***in My name***" (John 16:23). What does "in My name" mean? It does not mean what is so popularly believed, that if one adds the name "Jesus" to his prayers God will hear and answer and give him his request. The millions of unanswered prayers down the centuries of the existence of the Church should convince the sincere Christian that something is wrong with this interpretation.

The actual name "Jesus," whatever affectionate regard has been built up in our minds concerning it because of the loveliness of the Person who bears it, has no potency of itself. "Jesus" was one of the most common names amongst the Israelites. We do not see this because the word *Jesus* is Greek, derived from the Hebrew *Yeshua* (Joshua), both meaning *Savior*. There is an interesting translation in the King James version of the Bible where Stephen is made to say that "Jesus" brought in the Tabernacle with the Israelites into the Promised Land. The word, of course, should be "Joshua" (Acts 7:45). Many people named their children in those days after the great national hero, Joshua. When Paul and his company landed at Cyprus, and came to Paphos, Paul denounced a false prophet named "Bar Jesus" (Acts 13:6-12), whose name means "son of Jesus" (Greek), that is, "son of *Joshua*" (Hebrew).

There were certain men, including seven sons of a priest named Sceva, who tried the magic of the name "Jesus" upon a demoniac. Because of the many who were so named, they even made it clear *which* Jesus they meant—the "Jesus whom Paul preacheth." But it did not work. The evil spirit knew the Lord of glory, but not those who quoted His name; and these would-be exorcists had to flee from the demoniac, wounded and naked (Acts 19:13-16).

This very incident gives us **the key** to the truth of "in My name." *It all depends upon who says it—**not** upon the name quoted.* Jesus says, not that He will answer by virtue of His spoken name, but that the person asking the petition must be "in His name" when he makes his request. God has titles, but no name; all the names of God recorded in the Old Testament are descriptive titles—El, Elohim, El Shaddai, Jehovah, etc. God replied to Moses, when Moses asked for His name, "I AM THAT I AM" (Exodus 3:14). Moses knew all the titles by which God was then called, but was asking for His personal name. He has none. He is the glorious Original—the only One who has underived being. He has no need to be identified with a name, lest He be confused with other beings. A name was originally descriptive of the nature of the person bearing it. It is and will be forever impossible to condense all the many attributes of the Father, the Fount of Deity, the Most High and Eternal God, and express them in a single personal name.

> *And the* Lord *descended in the cloud, and stood with Moses there, and proclaimed the name of the* Lord. *[6]And the* Lord *passed by before him, and proclaimed, The* Lord, *the* Lord *God, merciful and gracious, longsuffering, and abundant in goodness and truth, [7]keeping mercy for thousands, forgiving iniquity and transgression and sin, and that will by no means clear the guilty....*
>
> *Exodus 34:5-7*

This is a major error of the so-called Jehovah's Witnesses, who claim that God's name is "Jehovah," and of the unitarian "Jesus only" people, who claim that the name of the Father, the Eternal One, and of the Holy Spirit is "Jesus"—a name given humanly to the Son (the Logos) when He came out of eternity into time upon this earth not long ago.

So if you are *in* Jesus, that is, *in His Person*, and you are a partaker of the Divine Nature; if your old man is crucified with Him,[3] self on the cross; if the Lord Jesus Christ is your all and your only desire; if Christ in you is the hope of glory;[4] if you are a vessel unto honor, sanctified and fit for the Master's use;[5] if you are a saint, not merely in name, but in deed and in truth—*then* because Christ is *in* you and you are *in* Him, your prayer comes up to the Father as Christ's own, and you shall ask what you will and it shall be done.

Such a person loves with the love of God; there is now no accusing conscience, for John says,

> *Beloved, if our heart condemn us not, then have we confidence toward God. [22]And whatsoever we ask, we receive of Him, because we keep His commandments, and do those things that are pleasing in His sight. [23]And this is His commandment, that we should believe on the name of His Son Jesus Christ, and love one another, as He gave us com-*

mandment. [24]And he that keepeth His commandments dwelleth in Him, and He in him. And hereby we know that He abideth in us, by the Spirit which He hath given us.

1 John 3:21-24

Such a person knows what the will of the Father is and asks only for those things that are His will.

And this is the confidence that we have in Him, that if we ask anything according to His will, He heareth us.

1 John 5:14

The one who desires to walk only with God, in the *nature* and *power* of God, may then consider what things he should ask for, and these things he will obtain. You are now aware that a mechanical belief in the Scriptures as a book of formulas from which one may choose does not get results. It was never the intention of God that it should be so; that is not the purpose of the collection and preservation, in God's will, of the Scriptures of Truth. The apostle Paul says, "For the kingdom of God is not in word but in power" (1 Corinthians 4:20), and, "For our gospel came not unto you in word only, but also in power and in the Holy Spirit and in much assurance" (1 Thessalonians 1:5).

Another Certainty: The Principle of *Desire*

The Word of the Lord is plain and clear: "He shall have *whatsoever.*" He gives no list from which one may choose. Yet not only must the *whatsoever* be according to the Father's will, but the one making the petition must truly desire it. There is so much in this word ***desire***. The original word means to "ask," but not to ask casually in the hope that the Father may perhaps grant the request. There are many thousands, nay millions, of unanswered prayers. Many persons have completely forgotten the prayers that once they prayed; that is one of the major reasons why the prayers were not answered. If we desire the thing for which we are asking to the extent that we shall never be satisfied unless we get it, then we shall eventually have that request for which we are making petition. He says that we must believe that our request is granted immediately. He does not say that what we are asking for is immediately ours. The words "shall have" have a hint of futurity about them; but the promise is certain and the answer sure.

God has much to say in Scripture concerning *desire*. David says, "One thing have I *desired* of the Lord, that will I seek after" (Psalm 27:4). One thing at a time, earnestly sought from God, will get for you an answer that will be surprising if you have been used to the prayer-list type of praying. *"One thing* have I desired, *that will I seek after."* Desire is an earnest, insatiable longing—not a whim, a wish, a fancy. The evidence of your desire is that you will seek after it. Consider a man who believes that he is thirsty; he says to his wife, "Honey, I think I feel thirsty. What shall I have to drink?" She says, "Well, there's hot coffee, or I'll boil some water for you and make a cup of tea (that would be in England), or there's orange drink or cola." He replies, "I don't fancy any of those." Is he *really* thirsty? Does he *desire* a drink? Consider another scene—a man, his face blackened by the sun, his lips cracked with thirst, his tongue swollen, his eyes bloodshot. He is in a wilderness of sand. Only one word ever escapes his tortured lips, only one thought engrosses his mind, only one thing is he seeking for—*water!* And he will seek until he drops exhausted and dies. *That* is *desire!* That is how some of us found the water of life; we felt that we would die unless we received it, and unlike the first man mentioned, we found that the Lord says,

"When the poor and needy seek water,
and there is none,
and their tongue faileth for thirst,
I the Lord will hear them,
I the God of Israel will not forsake them...
I will make the wilderness a pool of water."

Isaiah 41:17-18

God always responds to desire:

"Thou openest Thy hand
and satisfieth the ***desire*** *of every living thing."*

Psalm 145:16

It is the nature of His fatherhood to do so. He is universally the Father of His creation—He is the all-provider. He creates desire, and satisfies the desire of all His creatures.

"These all wait upon Thee;
that Thou mayest give them
their meat in due season."

Psalm 104:27

He satisfies all desire.

This truth, that God gives us the desire of our hearts, is sobering. Do be careful what you ask for with desire. What a need there is for us to be holy, that our desires may be the desires of the Spirit in us! It is one thing to be so much in the center of His purposes, to walk so closely with God, that His will is our will, and we can be instruments on earth of the Father's sovereign purposes—interceding with Him to do on earth what He desires and purposes to do. It is quite another thing to see that in the creative plan of God He has willed to fulfill the desires of the creatures that He has made. What an astonishing revelation of this truth we have in the subject of tithing. The Israelite was to tithe all of his increase and take the tithe to the place that the Lord had chosen (that is, where the Tabernacle would be), and share it there with the Levites in a great annual feast unto the Lord. *"If the way be too long for thee... then thou shalt turn it into money... and shalt go unto the place which the LORD thy God shall choose. And thou shalt bestow that money for whatsoever thy soul desireth, for oxen, or for sheep, or for wine, or for strong drink or for whatsoever thy soul desireth"* (Deuteronomy 14:22-27). One would have thought that the Lord would at least have cut the strong drink out, but He will not revoke His great decision concerning desire.

David reminds us that the children of Israel had a perverted desire for flesh, which they preferred to angel's food, manna (Psalm 78:25):

[They] lusted exceedingly in the wilderness
and tempted God in the desert,
and He gave them their request...

Psalm 106:14,15

He rained flesh also upon them as dust,
and feathered fowls like as the sand of the sea...
So they did eat, and were well filled;
for He gave them their own desire.

Psalm 78:27,29

They also received, says David, "leanness in their souls" (Psalm 106:15), and "the wrath of God came down upon them" (Psalm 78:31).

On another occasion the children of Israel wanted to be like the nations around them. They did not want the direct rule of God through one of His appointed judges; rather, they wanted to have a king of their own choosing. They were given a king whose name was Saul, and Samuel said, "Now therefore behold the king whom ye have chosen, and whom ye have *desired*" (1 Samuel 12:13). The history of the reign of Saul tells us the result of their wrong desire; but the desire was granted.

Even more were the Jews given their desire:

> *Now at the feast he [Pilate] released unto them one prisoner, whomsoever they desired.... And the multitude crying aloud began to desire him to do as he had ever done unto them.... And so Pilate, willing to content the people, released Barabbas unto them and delivered Jesus... to be crucified.*
>
> *Mark 15:6,8,15*

> *And he released unto them him that for sedition and murder was cast into prison, whom they had desired; but he delivered Jesus to their will.*
>
> *Luke 23:25*

This awful choice of desire is confirmed by Peter, who said,

> *But ye denied the Holy One and the Just, and desired a murderer to be granted unto you.*
>
> *Acts 3:14*

They chose a murderer and murder, rather than the Prince of Life and eternal life. The desire was not denied them; but has there ever been a people who have been more cruelly and ruthlessly murdered than the Jews? Be very, very careful what you thirst after, that is, what you desire.

Let Paul have the last word upon desire. He says, "We... do not cease to pray for you, and to desire that ye might be filled with the knowledge of His will in all wisdom and spiritual understanding; that ye might walk worthy of the Lord" (Colossians 1:9,10). Amen!

The Certainty of "This Is That"

There is a great difference between dogmatism and speaking with authority as a man of God. Dogmatism is the assertion of prejudiced self-will against obvious truth; "speaking with authority" is the assurance of one in the truth, who knows the truth. Only those who love the truth and are prepared to walk in it can discern the difference. One of the greatest certainties of faith is that the man of faith will be able to say, "This is that." At the feast of Pentecost, when the Holy Spirit fell upon the waiting disciples, Peter spoke with authority and said, "***This is that*** which was spoken by the prophet Joel" (Acts 2:16ff). If he had been a modern, theological scholar, he would have said, "It appears to me that this is that," or, "Could we not say that this is that?" or "I am almost convinced that this is that"; which would have meant that he was having quite a struggle against being convinced. He would have said alternatively, "Not to be dogmatic, I would suggest that this is that," and would have been very scornful of anyone who said, "This is that." Of course, he might even have rested on that comfortable, intellectual, theological cushion: "The general consensus of opinion amongst biblical scholars is that it is possible that this is that."

Why does Peter speak with such authority? Because he had just graduated (with dishonors) from a three-year course in God's Bible College under the personal tuition[6] of the Logos, the Everlasting Word. He had been humbled by chastisement; he had been purged from an evil heart of unbelief; his understanding had been opened so that he could understand the Scriptures; and he had been baptized in the Holy Spirit. He spoke by the inner witness of the Holy Spirit to truth.

Jesus had said, "When He, the Spirit of truth, is come, He will guide you into all truth" (John 16:13). John said, "It is the Spirit that beareth witness, because the Spirit is truth" (1 John 5:6). Those who walk with God in truth know the meaning of the Scripture, "He that believeth on the Son of God hath the witness in himself" (1 John 5:10). The baptism of the Holy Spirit under the New Covenant is not an experience that comes and goes. It is an implanted spring of living water that has come to stay. "He shall give you another Comforter (Greek: *parakletos—one called alongside to help*), that He might abide with you forever" (John 14:16). It is an anointing that *abides*. Special infillings of the Holy Spirit there will be for special service required from God; "but the anointing which ye have received of Him abideth in you, and ye need not that any man teach you: but as the same anointing teacheth you of all things, and is truth, and is no lie, and even as it hath taught you, ye shall abide in Him" (1 John 2:27). This does *not* mean that you have no need to be taught, for if that were so, the Lord Jesus would not have ordained teachers in His Church (Ephesians 4:11). Instead, it means that no one should be called "Rabbi" (teacher or master) upon the earth (Matthew 23:7-12); that is, you must be the disciple of no human being. If you are walking in the truth, and you hear something that purports to be the truth, the inner witness of the Spirit (if listened to) will confirm or reject it.

"This is that" is another of the great certainties of faith. "There was a man in Jerusalem, whose name was Simeon; and the same man was just and devout, waiting for the consolation of Israel: and the Holy Spirit was upon him" (Luke 2:25). It was revealed to this man by the Spirit that he should see the Lord's

Christ before his death (verse 26). When he saw the baby Jesus, he took Him up in his arms and said, "Lord, now lettest thou thy servant depart in peace... for mine eyes have seen Thy salvation" (verses 28-35). When he saw the Christ, he knew that this is that which was foretold to him and to many other prophets. "There was one Anna, a prophetess... and she coming in that instant gave thanks likewise unto the Lord, and spake of Him to all that looked for redemption in Jerusalem" (verses 36-38). She also knew that this is that.

We have today many contrary voices expounding prophetic interpretations; but none can say, "This is that." They have a different note, a human one—"this is going to be that" and, like all human things, it is not reliable. At the second coming of the Lord Jesus, it will not be an appearance of glory or a physical demonstration of wound-prints that will convince His true saints, for these things can be and have been imitated; rather it will be the inner witness of the abiding Comforter that "This is that" which He promised—"I will come again and receive you unto Myself" (John 14:3). This is the glorious final certainty of faith.

ENDNOTES FOR CHAPTER 8

1. Many Christians are unaware that it was a *Jewish* guard unit that stood watch at Jesus' tomb. This is why Pilate, in response to the Sanhedrin's request (Matthew 27:62-64), declares, "'*You* have a watch [i.e., a group of guards]; go *your* way, make it as secure as *you* can'" (verse 65); after which the very next verse notes, "So *they* went, and made the sepulchre sure, sealing the stone, and setting a watch" (verse 66).

   To what "watch" was Pilate referring? To the same body of Temple guards we encounter in such passages as John 7:32, 44-45; Acts 4:1; and Acts 5:22-24. Pilate had washed his hands of the whole affair (literally and figuratively—Matthew 27:24), so he was not about to assign any troops under his command to what he must have thought of as a "fool's errand." Thus he granted a special dispensation to the Jewish leaders, allowing their Temple guards to be stationed somewhere outside the Temple. It then follows that these same guards, when terrified by the angel (Matthew 28:4), fled in haste to their superiors, that is, to the Sanhedrin (verses 11-12), and received their orders from that body. Uncertain (because the situation of using the Temple guard outside of the Temple was unusual in Roman occupation) how Pilate might respond, the Sanhedrin declared that it would intervene if Pilate got wind of their dereliction of duty (verses 13-14). They said this knowing (as Pastor Gutteridge points out) that for a *Roman* soldier to fall asleep during guard duty, or to abandon his post for any reason, or to lose his prisoner, for whatever reason, would mean certain, unappealable execution (as happened in Acts 12:18-19). The council determined that it could be successfully argued that these Temple guards did not fall under the rules of Roman military jurisprudence, since they were neither Romans nor in the pay of the Roman army.

2. Recall chapter two, "The Conditions of Faith" pages 13-22.

3. This is alluding to Romans 6:6.

4. See Colossians 1:27.

5. As Paul says in 2 Timothy 2:21.

6. *Tuition*, in this context, means *instruction.*

·9·
The Inheritance of Faith

What shall I do my God to love,
My loving God to praise?
The length, and breadth, and height to prove,
And depth of sovereign grace?

Thy sovereign grace to all extends,
Immense and unconfined;
From age to age it never ends;
It reaches all mankind.

Throughout the world its breadth is known,
Wide as infinity;
So wide, it never passed by one,
Or it had passed by me.

My trespass was grown up to heaven;
But far above the skies,
In Christ abundantly forgiven,
I see Thy mercies rise.

The depth of all redeeming love,
What angel tongue can tell?
O may I to the utmost prove
The gift unspeakable![1]

—Charles Wesley—

THE FULFILLMENT OF THE GOSPEL is Christ in the heart. This is salvation; this is why He came, was born, suffered, died, and rose again. This is the purpose for which the Holy Spirit is given, to make the Lord Jesus Christ real in the heart.

> *That He would grant you, according to the riches of His glory, to be strengthened with might by His Spirit in the inner man; [17]that Christ may dwell in your hearts by faith; that ye, being rooted and grounded in love, [18]may be able to comprehend with all saints what is the **breadth** and **length** and **depth** and **height**; [19]and to know the love of Christ, which passeth knowledge, that ye might be filled with all the fulness of God.*
>
> *Ephesians 3:16-19*

For when the Holy Spirit has come, He gives the faith whereby the presence of Christ is an abiding experience, and because Christ is God and God is love, there is a rooting and grounding in love, so that from this root may grow by revelation an ever-increasing tree of knowledge of the exceeding love of God.

The Grace of Faith and the Gift of Faith

We must differentiate between:

- preternatural[2] faith, a quality of the divine nature which comes to us in the new birth, a *fruit* produced by the indwelling of the Holy Spirit—the *grace* of faith; and
- the essentially supernatural *gift* of faith.

The latter is given, in the sovereign will of the Holy Spirit, to those needing it for the fulfillment of a special task that He has chosen for them to do. This distinction is made clear in Scripture, which speaks of the fruit of faith in the epistle to the Galatians (5:22), and of the gift of faith in 1 Corinthians 12:9. They are usually designated "the grace of faith" and "the gift of faith."

God gave this special gift of faith to George Müller.[3] It enabled him to believe that every need would be provided for the many orphans put under his care. Dr. A. T. Pierson, in his *George Muller of Bristol,* mentions that this truth was revealed to Müller through an experience of suffering which he went through in 1832. He had the misfortune to break a blood-vessel the day before the Sunday when he had to preach at three chapel services. Dr. Pierson says:

> After an hour of prayer, he felt that faith was given him to rise, dress and go to the chapel; and though very weak... he was helped to preach as usual, growing stronger rather than weaker with each effort. When a medical friend remonstrated, he replied that he should himself have regarded it as presumptuous had not the Lord given him the faith... He himself did not always pursue a like course, because he had not always a like faith, and this leads him in his journal to draw a valuable distinction between the gift of faith and the grace of faith.[4]

The Dimensions of Our Inheritance

The commencement of the entering into our inheritance through faith is while we are yet living upon earth. Before ever we mount to the skies, we begin to enter into the riches of our inheritance. Here then is a revelation, unknown and therefore unappreciated by those who are not the children of God, but to us who are the called according to His purpose, of exquisite preciousness. See how Paul unfolds it in the third chapter of Ephesians.

- The ***breadth***—Not only the Jews, but also the Gentiles should be fellow-heirs, and of the same body, and partakers of God's promise in Christ by the gospel (Ephesians 3:6). "Unto me... is this grace given, that I should preach among the Gentiles the unsearchable riches of Christ" (verse 8). Even this is hardly broad enough for Paul. He completes it by saying, "And to make all men see what is the fellowship of the mystery, which from the beginning of the world hath been hid in God, who created all things by Jesus Christ" (verse 9).

- That very verse introduces us also to the ***length*** which, to be measured accurately, must begin "from the beginning of the world" (verse 9). We shall need an infinite measuring tape, because it unrolls to God's glory "in the Church... throughout all ages, world without end" (verse 21).

- How can we plumb the ***depth*** of the love of God? There is only one satisfying and complete revelation of the depth of the Father's love: it was when He gave His Son, who most willingly came down an immeasurable depth, down through the *cherubim*, past the *seraphim*, past the principalities and powers, lower yet—past the archangels and angels, still lower—through the azure floor of Heaven, down to earth. Lower yet He came, passing by kings and presidents, dukes and earls, lords, rich men and captains, to take the form of a servant, and to be obedient unto death, even the death of the cross. All we can do is *state* the extent of the depth; we can never *comprehend* it.

- To view the ***height*** of the love of God, one must stand upon earth, look toward Heaven, and see that God has chosen to give the principalities and powers in those heavenly places a new lesson in the profundity of His wisdom, by the revelation of the Church (verse 10), which is the body of Christ and the fullness of Him, the Head, that fills all in all.

This is an inheritance indeed, and one that we begin to enter into on earth, as Christ, by the Spirit, abides in our hearts through faith. But always, the best is yet to be. "Looking unto Jesus the author and finisher of our faith, who for the joy that was set before Him endured the cross, despising the shame, and is set down at the right hand of the throne of God" (Hebrews 12:2). It would be foolish to doubt our faith, for Jesus is its Author. It would be foolish to fear that in the end we shall be overcome by doubt and lose it, for Jesus is its Finisher. He is the Alpha and the Omega, the first and the last; and He will perform and finish what He has begun.

There is a time coming when we shall be the *manifested* sons of God. At present the Church is an invisible church. Now the sons of God are not visible as His sons; they appear in the same physical form as the sons of Adam. Nor can they be revealed until He, the Son, is revealed; for how can there be visible sons when *the* Son is invisible? It is the will of God that the true Church as an entity should not yet be known to mankind as "the Church"; no one can say, "Lo here!" or "Lo, there!" (Luke 17:21) about either the Head—Jesus—or the body—the Church. Although the Church has been plagued throughout all of its existence, even to the present day, by sectarians claiming that their exclusive group is the whole church, still the word of the Founder and Head holds true: "Where two or three are gathered together in My name, there am I in the midst of them" (Matthew 18:20).

Wisdom should teach us that one cannot have an invisible head and a visible body. While Christ—our Head—is invisible, the Church—His body—will be invisible; and "when Christ who is our life, shall appear, then shall ye also appear with Him in glory" (Colossians 3:4). John makes this very clear: "Beloved, now are we the sons of God, and it doth not yet appear what we shall be." One would think that this would be conclusive evidence that the manifestation of the sons of God is yet to come, as indeed, John goes on to say: "But we know that when He shall appear, we shall be like Him, for we shall see Him as He is" (1 John 3:2).

Elisha: A Type of Persistent Faith

The greatest reward of faith is in the future; but there is also an inheritance that persistent faith may enter into here and now. There are those who long to be the heirs of the prophets, to have the "double portion," that is, the birthright blessing; and these shall obtain it. The great example of this truth, given for our instruction in the biblical record, is that of Elijah and Elisha (2 Kings 2). Elisha had one all-embracing, God-inspired desire, and that was to inherit Elijah's office. He wanted to be his heir. In those days a father divided his property among his sons into a number of equal parts, but with one more part than he had sons. The eldest son, who had the birthright blessing, had in addition to his own portion this extra one. This is the "double portion" asked for by Elisha. What he is requesting is to be Elijah's heir. The strange reply of that prophet was that only if he were present when Elijah was taken away would he receive that inheritance (verse 10).

There were two things alone that could testify that Elisha had received this promise: Elijah's mantle, which was the *out-*

ward and visible insignia of the office; and Elijah's spirit, which was the *internal and invisible motive force* of all his mighty deeds. Only Elisha's persistent and unswerving walk of faith could make these blessings his. Why should it be that Elisha would only receive his request if he were present when Elijah was taken up? Because if Elisha were an actual witness of Elijah's translation, he could forever testify that Elijah was not dead, but living.

This was the great testimony of the apostles, that the Lord Jesus was not dead, but alive. It was a most necessary qualification of the Twelve who were especially called the "Twelve apostles of the Lamb" (Revelation 21:14). There were other apostles, such as Paul, Barnabas, and Silas; but these were not of the Twelve. Peter said,

> *Wherefore of these men which have companied with us all the time that the Lord Jesus went in and out among us... must one be ordained to be a witness with us of His resurrection... and the lot fell upon Matthias, and he was numbered with the eleven apostles.*
>
> *Acts 1:21-26*

These Twelve are to have a special office in the Millennium. Jesus said to them, "When the Son of Man shall sit in the throne of His glory, ye also shall sit upon twelve thrones, judging the twelve tribes of Israel" (Matthew 19:28). They were essentially witnesses ***of*** the resurrection of the Lord Jesus; later apostles and disciples would witness ***to*** His resurrection.

Elisha followed his master from Gilgal to Bethel, from Bethel to Jericho, and from Jericho to Jordan and the wilderness. He survived all the testings that Elijah put upon him; he refused to abide in any of the spiritual experiences that he came into; his ever-increasing faith saw that these were but steps to the goal, not the goal itself. Very few Christians are like Elisha, for they arrive at a spiritual plateau up the mountain and, being content with that, do not press on to the summit. They are saved from hell and are satisfied, or they go a little further and speak in tongues and are content, or they enter into a measure of victory, and rest therein; but the goal of being in the character and power of their Beloved, and of having the exceeding joy and privilege of following the Lamb "whithersoever He goeth," is not their overwhelming and only desire. These will never inherit the "double portion" as Elisha did, for "Elijah went up by a whirlwind into heaven, *and Elisha saw it*" (2 Kings 2:11,12). Therefore he inherited Elijah's mantle; "he took up also the mantle of Elijah that fell from him" (verse 13). He also received Elijah's spirit: "When the sons of the prophets... saw him, they said, 'The spirit of Elijah doth rest on Elisha' " (verse 15).

Christ's Mantle: His Perfect Nature

This is the great secret of the apostolic testimony, and of ours, too, if by patient endurance in steadfast faith we will walk with God. "And with great power gave the apostles witness of the resurrection of the Lord Jesus" (Acts 4:33). So they inherited by right two things—Christ's mantle and His Spirit. His mantle is represented by His seamless dress, which is His nature, His righteousness, His perfect, spotless holiness that is completely without seam or flaw. Just as "the coat was without seam, woven from *the top* throughout" (John 19:23), so His perfection of holiness came down with Him from above. He did not have to acquire it or attain to it.

This the apostles had, by the gift of God, not in the same infinite degree as the Christ, but of the same quality. They made no excuse for sin; they even called upon Christians to observe their apostolic behavior and to copy them. Paul says, "Be ye followers of me, even as I also am of Christ" (1 Corinthians 11:1). Also, "Those things which ye have both learned and received and heard and seen in me do: and the God of peace shall be with you" (Philippians 4:9). They recognized that the Lord had done a mighty work ***in*** them, as well as ***for*** them; they had a real salvation.

It would be well to observe here that the apostles were not supermen; their modern representatives are not princes of the church who have costly ecclesiastical dress and pomp and political power, but with little spiritual power. In apostolic days there were no princes of the church. We have already pointed out that the apostles had no distinctive dress, style, or appearance, and it was exceptional if one of them, such as Paul, had education. The educated men of the time "perceived that they [the Apostles] were unlearned and ignorant men" (Acts 4:13). They had received the double gift that their Lord had obtained for them—

1. *before* God by faith—Christ their righteousness;

2. *within* them by faith—Christ their holiness.

They were not novel exceptions; they were just samples of the Church for which the Lord Jesus had given Himself *"that He might sanctify and cleanse it with the washing of water by the word, that He might present it to Himself a glorious church, not having spot or wrinkle or any such thing, but that it should be holy and without blemish"* (Ephesians 5:26,27). The Christian standard of conduct in those days, untrammeled by subsequent human theories excusing sin, could be briefly summarized as: Having faults? Yes! Guilty of sin? No!

Christ's Spirit: Power and Holiness

The apostles also had—being witnesses of Christ's resurrection—His Spirit, freely conferred upon them, enabling them to continue their Lord's ministry of deliverance that He had commenced when He announced "The Spirit of the Lord is upon Me, because He hath anointed Me... to preach deliverance" (Luke 4:18). This was a ministry in power, with miracles and signs. Peter confirms that power and holiness are the two insignia that should mark not only the pioneers, the apostles, but every follower of the Lamb. He said, "Why look ye so earnestly on us, as though by our own power or holiness we had made this man to walk?" (Acts 3:12) Power and holiness are never separated in a true experience wrought by the sovereign Holy Spirit; they are the celestial stamp, the Divine hallmark, which accompanies every true revival of religion. Nor can one distinguish a line of demarcation between the two, for both proceed from One—the sanctifying Spirit of almighty power.

There will occur variations in doctrinal conceptions accompanying revivals, but the product is always the same—transformed men and women with supernatural spiritual power and holiness. Where either of these becomes the emphasis (as after some time one or the other usually does), there is degeneracy, on the one hand, into an unhealthy interest in supernatural manifestations, and, on the other hand, into superior, legal self-righteousness, misnamed holiness. The Holy Spirit is not the monopoly of any denomination, and where such a people attempt to corner Him as their sole possession, to the despising of others who it is believed have not the same light or experience, the anointing has already left them. The almighty Spirit will not dwell in a temple made with hands. Your doctrinal beliefs, although founded upon Scripture, can never make a cage to confine that Holy Dove. Those earliest, faithful disciples of Jesus, ready to seal their testimony with their blood, had the authority (Greek: *exousia*) that ever goes with the nature of divine sonship, and the power (Greek: *dunamis*) that ever accompanies the presence of the Holy Ghost.

Full Salvation

All will be fully restored to the Church before the Divine clock has chimed the hour of midnight, or ever the new dawn comes when "the Sun of Righteousness shall arise with healing in His wings" (Malachi 4:2). Now is the time to realize what God's salvation is. It is not just an escape from hell! Devout Cornelius had no idea what the extent of salvation was when the angel said "that Peter would tell him words whereby thou and all thy house shall be saved" (Acts 11:14), but he discovered to his amazement that it included belief in Jesus and His resurrection, forgiveness of sins, the gift of the Holy Spirit, a new tongue, and a pure heart. "If thou shalt confess with thy mouth the Lord Jesus and shalt believe in thy heart that God hath raised Him from the dead, thou shalt be saved" (Romans 10:9).

Are you a witness that Jesus is alive? that He is ascended? that He is ever present by His Spirit to do all that ever He once did on earth? Then you may have by inheritance two things: His seamless mantle and His Spirit. But "I will yet for this be enquired of... to do it for them," saith the Lord GOD (Ezekiel 36:37). See your privilege. Once when He was on earth, they pressed to *touch* the hem of His garment; but you may *wear* it! Are you willing to come the Elisha way of persevering faith, that you may share this heirship of Christ? God will not separate the two; it is not "either/or," for Elijah's mantle is of no use without Elijah's spirit. He will not let you manifest the true Gifts of the Spirit without your cultivation by grace of the Fruits of the Spirit; Jesus said, "Ye shall know them by their fruits" (Matthew

7:16), *not* by "their gifts." And the Divine Husbandman will not produce His fruit in you without also giving, by His Spirit, His supernatural gifts. You despise either at your peril. Elisha did not work in two separate compartments of his nature; he was a harmonious whole.

Elisha's two first miracles are proof of this truth of supernatural power and holiness. He took up the mantle and said, "Where is the God of Elijah"—the God of fire, of miracles, of judgment (2 Kings 2:14)? He then smote the Jordan and it divided, as it had done at the command of Elijah. His next miracle was an invisible deed of cleansing, a type of the cleansing of the human heart (2 Kings 2:19-22). The city of Jericho had been under a curse ever since the days of Joshua, who had said, "Cursed be the man before the LORD that riseth up and buildeth this city Jericho" (Joshua 6:26). The men of the city came to Elisha and said, "The situation of this city is pleasant... but the water is bad and the land is unfruitful." The curse was present in the water; so the land was barren and the cattle kept casting their young.

This is a type of humanity. God declares that "the heart is deceitful above all things and desperately wicked" (Jeremiah 17:9). The Lord Jesus confirmed this when he said, "For from within, out of the heart of men, proceed evil thoughts, adulteries, fornications, murders, thefts, covetousness, wickedness, deceit, lasciviousness, an evil eye, blasphemy, pride, foolishness; all these evil things come from within" (Mark 7:21-23). It is the presence of these things in the heart that causes barrenness in the spiritual life.

Elisha took a new cruse and "went forth unto the spring of the waters, and cast the salt in there and said, 'Thus saith the LORD, "I have healed these waters; there shall not be from thence any more death or barren land" ' " (2 Kings 2:21). This is what the Lord does with the heart; the purifying work of the

Holy Spirit is shown in the cleansing, preserving nature of the salt. Wise Elisha went to the spring of the waters, cleansing the water at its source. And that is what the Lord does, cleansing the heart from whence, as He says, the evil has been flowing. It was a new cruse that Elisha took, for we have this blessing under the New Covenant.

The Bible also speaks of the same experience under another figure: *"The LORD thy God will circumcise thine heart, and the heart of thy seed, to love the LORD thy God with all thine heart, and with all thy soul"* (Deuteronomy 30:6). Stephen, inspired by the Holy Spirit, reproached the Jews: *"Ye stiffnecked and uncircumcised in heart and ears, ye do always resist the Holy Ghost"* (Acts 7:51). This word cut them to the heart, but they proved the truth of it. The murder in their hearts leaped out at Stephen and they stoned him to death. Stephen would not have accused them of having an uncircumcised heart if he had had one himself. As with Cornelius and his fellow Gentiles, as with Peter and the disciples of the Upper Room, God-given faith and the tongue of flame that came down with the Holy Spirit had purified his heart. He had, under the New Covenant, a new heart.

The God of Elijah is the God of our Lord Jesus Christ, and He will do far more exceeding abundantly above all that you ask or even think (Ephesians 3:20). Go to the Lord, if you would inherit these blessings, and not to a man! A man might well deny a truth beyond his own experience. Those who seek from the Lord, with an honest heart, in persistent faith, will possess these great inheritances of faith.

ENDNOTES FOR CHAPTER 9

---

1. From Wesley's hymn, ***Infinite, Unexhausted Love***, found in one page 199.

---

2. *Preternatural:* existing outside of nature; inexplicable by ordinary means

3. Depending on the author, the name is spelled variously as Muller, Mueller, and Müller. Except for the title of Pierson's book, we have settled on *Müller*, since it is the spelling which appears on his tombstone in Arnos Vale Cemetery, Bristol, England. (Note also that there is another title version of Pierson's work called *George Mueller of Bristol and His Witness to a Prayer-Hearing God.*)
4. *George Mueller of Bristol*, pp. 88,89

·10· The Triumph of Faith

FAITH IS THE SUBSTANCE that cements us to all the promises of God, the sweet bond of union that assures to us our abiding in the love of the Father. Faith leads us on to eventual triumph. *"Who shall separate us from the love of Christ?... For I am persuaded that neither death, nor life, nor angels, nor principalities, nor powers, nor things present, nor things to come, nor height, nor depth, nor any other creature, shall be able to separate us from the love of God, which is in Christ Jesus our Lord"* (Romans 8:35-39). God has appointed the way whereby we may obtain all of His promises: it is the way of faith. The Lord Jesus once said to a man of a doubting heart, "Believe! All things are possible to him that believeth" (Mark 9:23).

Faith is the arm of the electric trolley-bus that, pressing upon the overhead wires, brings the power down. Faith is Franklin's kite soaring up into the heavens, conveying the awful power of the lightning to earth. Faith is Moses' arms stretched up to God, assuring victory for Israel. Faith reaches far up into the invisible and brings down the almighty resources of God. Paul is on a sinking ship, the hold awash, the timbers starting,[1] all masts long gone by the board; but up goes Paul's right arm of faith and, holding on with the other to the stump of a jury mast, he says, "Sirs, be of good cheer: for I believe God" (Acts 27:25). No one on the ship could drown after that.

What boundless resources are at the disposal of faith – "the unsearchable riches of Christ," as Paul calls them in Ephesians 3:8. Those riches include:

- riches of *power:* "All power is given unto Me in heaven and in earth" (Matthew 28:18);
- riches of *wealth:* "The silver is mine and the gold is mine, saith the Lord of Hosts" (Haggai 2:8);
- riches of *boundless supply:* "My God shall supply all your need, according to His riches in glory by Christ Jesus" (Philippians 4:19).

There is nothing beyond the reach of faith.

Faith does not consider the possibility of defeat. The devil cannot win even one battle, for Christ achieved everlasting victory on Calvary. Good Mr. Feeble-mind, of the *Pilgrim's Progress,* was taken by giant Slay-good, and although the giant had him in his clutches and was preparing to pick his bones, yet even Mr. Feeble-mind still believed that somehow all would be well. He said, upon his rescue,

> *I believed I should come out alive again; for I have heard, that not any pilgrim that is taken captive by violent hands, if he keeps heart-whole towards His Master, is by the laws of Providence, to die by the hand of the enemy.*

Faith knows that guardian angels are always closer than the hosts of Midian,[2] and that because the Head, in Heaven, is seated upon the throne of the universe, then the body, the Church, is joined with Him there (Ephesians 2:6).

Introducing Enoch and His Era

There is to be a final triumph of faith, and we shall close this book with the Lord's great encouragement and solemn warning given to us in the example of Enoch. "By faith, Enoch was translated that he should not see death, and was not found because God had translated him; for before his translation, he had this testimony, that he pleased God" (Hebrews 11:5). Enoch is the Lord's earliest example of triumphant faith. The Bible record is, "And Enoch walked with God, and he was not; for God took him" (Genesis 5:24). Enoch was the seventh generation from Adam. Jude says:

> *And Enoch also, the seventh from Adam, prophesied of these, saying, "Behold, the Lord cometh with ten thousand of His saints, [15]to execute judgment upon all, and to convince all that are ungodly among them of all their ungodly deeds which they have ungodly committed, and of all their hard speeches which ungodly sinners have spoken against Him."*
>
> *Jude 14-15*

Enoch knew Adam well; he knew him for three hundred and eight years, for Adam died only about fifty years before Enoch's translation. Adam lived for nine hundred and thirty years (Genesis 5:5), and he was six hundred and twenty-two years old when Enoch was born. Adam knew Methuselah, the living example of God's grace, the man who lived to the greatest age of any man, and who died as his name had indicated,[3] just before the judgment of the universal Deluge. Adam also saw Lamech, who was Noah's father. Adam used to listen to Enoch's prophecies, and knew very much more about them than we do. He heard Enoch give the only authentic word, quoted above, that has come down to us. It is the only genuine prophecy of Enoch, borrowed to give the apocryphal book of Enoch the stamp of authenticity; but the Holy Spirit has preserved it for us in the inspired letter of Jude. Enoch had, from Adam, a first-hand account of the Garden of Eden; and he learned as much about the Creation as Adam knew. He often listened to Adam describing the glories of the Garden, and must have shed sympathetic tears as he heard about the tragedy of the Fall.

In Enoch's days and during the last days of Adam, things were drawing to a climax. Whenever judgment is impending, two things happen: God seeks to revive His people; and the evil one brings a strange apathy over humanity. No one seems to care anymore about the future. What were the conditions of Enoch's days? There was some knowledge of what, in God's sight, constituted morality. It was inherited from Adam, and conscience testified to it. But there was no check on moral conduct, for everyone, except the very few righteous, took each other's conduct as the standard. It was a permissive society! The original revelation was drawing out thinner and thinner as the years went by. It had become attenuated by the increasing distances as the human race spread out. Nevertheless, no one doubted special creation; no one doubted the existence of God. No one believed in the theory of organic evolution, that is, that life had come by chance. The idea had not yet been invented. All knew that life had originated in the sole Author of life—God.

Everyone except a very, very few, the righteous, accepted the doctrine of *uniformitarianism*, that is, that there had been and would continue to be an essential uniformity of cause and effect concerning the physical history of the world since creation; so no cataclysm could occur. Of course, very shortly their theory was in for a rude shock; but it was a nice, comfortable doctrine to excuse sin and lull the conscience, until it was suddenly shattered. No one doubted that God was somewhere, but they guessed that He had left the earth and was no longer concerned with it. He had gotten it going, but then He had left it to look after itself. After all, one had only to look up and see the great revolving macrocosm of the universe (and eyes were sharper and the atmosphere clearer then) to know that He had quite enough to concern Himself with up there; so they said, "Make the best of things. Do as you like. Have a good time. Enjoy yourself!"

The Lord *had* withdrawn Himself; He would not be present amid the deeds of blood and lust and crime. Once He had walked with Adam and Eve in the Garden. Even after sin had entered into the world, He was still present. Men knew the place where He could be found, for Cain had talked with Him until he "went out from the presence of the LORD" (Genesis 4:16). By the time of Enos, the grandson of Adam, there was no place where He could be found; "then began men to call upon the name of the LORD" (Genesis 4:26).

Spiritualism was rife in those days, but not the kind that satisfies the much lower intelligence of many today. They did not hold hands in darkened rooms or play with luminous paint, ouija boards, or toy trumpets; the evil spirit intelligences of today have matched themselves to the degeneracy of modern minds. Openly and unashamedly, in those days, people held communication with spirit beings. They had been used to angels as messengers of God. All knew of the *cherubim* who with flaming sword guarded for a time the tree of life, until God removed it (Genesis 3:24).

Now, in their rebellion, men welcomed the fallen intelligences, the friends of Lucifer, which assumed physical form and had intercourse with earth's women, who in those early days were exceedingly fair of form; and children were born to them, giants and mighty men, men of renown (Genesis 6:4). Every nation has its myths and legends of giants and heroes. The Greeks, who especially preserved and tabulated these things, are a fair example of the whole. The Titans, the Centimanni, and the Cyclops are specimens of the giants, as are also Anak (Numbers 13:22, 28,33), Og (Deuteronomy 3:1-4,10-13), and Goliath (1 Samuel 17), mentioned in the Bible, who came later. Perseus, the slayer of the Gorgon Medusa, was the son of the father of the gods, Zeus, and the earth maiden Danae. Hercules, renowned for his strength, was the son of Zeus and the woman Alcmene. The gods of the Greeks and Romans were uninhibited libertines, as their numerous children by earth women, whom they raped freely, testify. What to fallen man was a wonder and an action to admire and copy, to the Most Holy One and His few worshippers on earth was a most awful and shameful thing. God shut up these offending angelic beings in Tartarus,[4] as revealed by Peter (2 Peter 2:4) and also by Jude (verse 6), and bound them with everlasting chains against the Judgment Day.[5]

Wherever man had gone, violence had gone with him. "The earth was filled with violence" (Genesis 6:13). Murder had become a matter of amusement and of entertainment, of boasting and pride, as the speech of Lamech to his two wives reveals (Genesis 4:23,24).

"All flesh had corrupted its way" (Genesis 6:12); that is, all living things were becoming perverted from the original purpose of God. At the lowest end of the scale of creation, beneficent bacteria had become malignant germs of disease; insects having the gift of a sharp instrument useful for many purposes, such as the piercing of the bark of a tree in order to lay an egg in the incision, began to use it in attack, venomously, to sting and to cause harm. Winged flies, made to exhibit their grace and beauty, degenerated into repulsive spreaders of disease; others, formed to nourish their bodies upon the sap of plants, began to suck blood; and so upward in the ascending order of nature, as herbivorous animals became carnivores, and by reason of the amazing virility of those earliest times, developed teeth adapted to their new diet. At the head of the animal kingdom, its fallen god, man, was now producing demi-celestials, giants, and monsters.

Bigamy, leading eventually to polygamy and the inevitable subjugation of woman as the possession of the man, had begun. Lamech, of the line of Cain, had two wives, Adah and Zillah (Genesis 4:19-24). Man, more physically powerful than but not mentally superior to woman, was leading the universal trend of rule by force and violence, as opposed to rule by justice and law; so woman was becoming man's slave and thing. In the beginning it was not so. There was an equality between Adam and Eve. Eve was Adam's helpmeet (the word in Genesis 2:18 means *partner*), and by reason of her sin and the Fall, the Lord God said, "Thy desire shall be to thy husband, and he shall rule over thee" (Genesis 3:16). But in Christ all is restored: the wife is again restored to liberty (but not independence), and husband and wife are one as partners again (1 Peter 3:7; Galatians 3:28).

God's Dealings: Saving *From* and *Through* Tribulation

It was at this time, and under these conditions, that God prepared Enoch for translation. The reader who has followed closely the preceding brief outline of the conditions of the earth prior to the Noachian[6] Deluge will have seen that very similar conditions obtain at the present day. It was during this time that the Lord God, who had led Enoch to walk by faith with Him through this evil scene, prepared him for his final triumph—rapture.

Jesus said, "And as it was in the days of Noah, so shall it be also in the days of the Son of man" (Luke 17:26). How did the Lord deal with His people then? That is exactly how He will deal with them now. Enoch He saved ***from*** the tribulation of the Deluge by rapturing him; Noah and his family He saved ***through***, but *not from*, that tribulation. The wicked suffered fully in the Deluge tribulation. God gave Enoch the opportunity to qualify for translation, and Enoch walked by faith with God and fulfilled it. The very words of the Lord Jesus concerning the judgments which would overtake the world before His coming, and the promise of escape to the watchful ones, equally applied to the generation before the Flood: "Watch ye therefore, and pray always, that ye may be accounted worthy to escape all these things that shall come to pass, and to stand before the Son of Man" (Luke 21:36). Enoch alone was found worthy to escape, and he was raptured well before the fountains of the great deep were broken up and the windows of heaven were opened.

Two Kinds of Tribulation

There are two kinds of tribulation that can beset mankind; one is caused by the wrath of man, and the other, far more awful, is a manifestation of the wrath of God. Both of these are mentioned and differentiated in the first chapter of the second letter of Paul to the church at Thessalonica. He speaks first of the necessity and the subsequent reward of enduring with patience the wrath of man.

> *We ourselves glory in you in the churches of God for your patience and faith in all your persecutions and tribulations that ye endure, [5]Which is a manifest token of the righteous judgment of God, that ye may be counted worthy of the kingdom of God, for which ye also suffer.*
>
> *2 Thessalonians 1:4-5*

This is tribulation caused by the wrath and malice of man, inspired by the evil one who hates the people of God. The Lord has not promised to protect His people from such suffering, and has often allowed them to endure it. Then Paul goes on to speak of divine judgments:

> *Seeing it is a righteous thing with God to recompense tribulation to them that trouble you; [7]and to you who are troubled rest with us, when the Lord Jesus shall be revealed from heaven with His mighty angels, [8]in flaming fire taking vengeance on them that know not God....*
>
> *2 Thessalonians 1:6-8*

From this series of judgments, culminating in the descent of the Lord Jesus from Glory, God would save His people. Notice that it is the "righteous judgment of God" (verse 5) that the Church should endure that tribulation through persecution that refines it; this has been the lot of the Church from its earliest days. It is also "a righteous thing with God" (verse 6) that tribulation should be recompensed to them who have caused the Church to suffer. The Church is the body, the Lord Jesus is the Head; so just as He endured suffering by the assaults of men, so must the Church—for body and Head are all one. But all judgment has been committed to the Son (John 5:22), and the most awful anger is the wrath of the Lamb, far more terrible than the wrath of the lion, the devil.

It is impossible that the Church should endure that final manifestation of destructive wrath; could He punish His own body? There must be a way of escape for the Church. The Lord always makes provision for His people; but He makes a difference between them. Those who wholly follow the Lord are saved *from* His judgments. They are not present when the vials of His wrath are poured out. Those who are not utterly consecrated are saved *in* and *through* the judgments; they are present, but not hurt by them.

Examples of *Through* and *From*

Consider these examples:

Israel and Jethro

When God would punish the Egyptians and execute judgment upon all the gods of Egypt, then His people, being present, saw all of His awful works and were in much fear, but were kept safely in the land of Goshen. Israel in great trembling was taken dry-shod through the sea that was soon to break over the heads of Pharaoh and his hosts, to their utter destruction. Then Israel, in safety, on the very borders of that destroying sea, sang the triumph song of Moses. Yet, at the same time, Jethro, the priest of Midian, who had never lived in luxurious Egypt but had been content to serve his God in the desert, was living in peace and safety with his family, far from the sight and sound of judgment.

Lot and Abraham

When God decided to destroy Sodom and Gomorrah with fire from the heavens, He saved just Lot and as many of his family as would listen to him (Genesis 19:1-17); and they all, trembling and afraid, fled to Zoar which He specially spared (at Lot's request) to be a refuge for him (verses 18-23). Lot did not walk with God in faith, and he could not believe the word of God that he was safe in Zoar, so he fled to the mountains (verse 30).

Meanwhile, the man of faith who lived apart from that wicked, sinful world—Abraham, the friend of God—knew, by revelation, the purposes of God, and talked with Him of His judgments. Abraham was in perfect peace and confidence, far from the presence of destruction, while Lot was fleeing in terror. Both were righteous men, but one was sanctified to God, lived apart from the world, and had a pure heart toward God; the other did not. "Abraham gat up early in the morning to the place where he stood before the LORD" (Genesis 19:27), and shortly afterward he received the gift of a son, Isaac, by miraculous birth; while at the same time, Lot, made drunk, was living incestuously with his unbelieving daughters, who gave birth to children of the flesh, Moab and Ammon (Genesis 19:30-38), whose descendants became the enemies of the heirs of Abraham, the man of consecration and faith.

Noah and Enoch

It is significant that Enoch was raptured away from the place of judgment, but Noah was present with his family through that most awful time, tossed upon waves thousands of feet high, shut in with squealing, barking, roaring, malodorous (there were two skunks in the ark), frightened animals, but safe; just as Israel was safe and Lot was safe. But there had been a better way. Israel's sin of unbelief was revealed during their pilgrimage in the desert. Lot's sin we have referred to. Noah's lack of complete consecration was shown, like Lot's, by the sin of drunkenness and subsequent display of the flesh (Genesis 9:20-21).

The Siege of Jerusalem, 70 A.D.

Consider that when the time of judgment came to Jerusalem, those Christians who had sacrificed all in utter consecration to the Lord and who had obeyed His word, going out into all the world to preach the Gospel, were far away when the destroying armies of Rome were beginning to encircle the city. The fate of Jerusalem in A.D. 70 was so awful that the graphic pen of Josephus[7] can give us only some faint glimpse of the horrors of that time. Within Jerusalem, clinging sentimentally to the doomed city, bound by tradition, by position, by religion, by friendly but unchristian neighbors, were Christians, truly in the Lord's body. He made provision for them as He had promised (Mark 13:14); the Roman armies, strangely under the control of Divine providence, drew back for a short time, enabling the Christians to flee in safety to Pella, in the mountains. Once again the Lord saved His people from His wrath, as He had Noah, Lot, and Israel, though they were in the very midst of judgment; but He saved Enoch, Abraham, and Jethro from even the presence of His wrath.

Enoch's Preparation for Rapture

We must now look at the life of Enoch and see how he was prepared for rapture, and so escaped the presence of the judgment. He did not qualify apart from the grace of God. It is one thing to attempt to be pure and holy by the effort of the flesh, which is impossible; it is quite another thing to be pure and holy by faith, through grace, and by an obedient ear to the still, small voice of the Holy Spirit. God would not call us to be holy if it were not possible. It is unbelief in the heart which attempts to repudiate this truth.

This triumph of faith is not by means of a final act of faith, but it is the culmination of the walk of faith with God. One cannot walk with God except by invitation. The Lord Jesus called His disciples individually to walk with Him. He said to each one, "Come, follow Me!"—and each one who was willing arose and followed Him. This following Him in discipleship is neither mechanical in its thinking nor automatic in its action. One can refuse to follow Him. *The will must respond to the grace which has extended the call.* The Lord Jesus gave exactly the same call to the rich young ruler, who refused it. "Then Jesus... said to him, 'Come, take up the cross and follow Me.' And he was sad at that saying, and went away grieved" (Mark 10:21,22). The call of

Christ is evidenced by an internal desire to follow Him. The enemy reacts by inciting the fear of all the dangers and unpleasant things that will result from the call. Grace makes the will free to decide, and the human will—not compulsive Divine pressure—gives the deciding choice. The Almighty God *could*, but does not, turn stones into the children of Abraham (Matthew 3:9; Luke 3:8). All of His children will be with Him in Heaven by free choice, not because they were subject to an irresistible and inescapable destiny. For this reason, the Lord Jesus Christ in the day of judgment will justly punish those who *could* have followed but would not, and will reward those who could have turned back but did not.

We must take up our cross if we would walk with God, "looking unto Jesus, the Author and finisher of our faith, who for the joy that was set before Him endured the cross, despising the shame" (Hebrews 12:2). The way of the cross may be the way of sorrow, but it is also the way of joy. The antonym of *joy* is not *sorrow*, but *misery*; sorrow and joy are compatible. Sorrow is one of the wisest of God's teachers.

I walked a mile with Pleasure;
She chattered all the way,
Nor left me ought the wiser
For all she had to say.

I walked a mile with Sorrow,
And ne'er a word said she,
But oh! the things I learned from her,
When Sorrow walked with me.[8]

—Robert Browning Hamilton—

When the rich, young ruler refused the Lord's call to take up his cross and follow, he went away full of grief. If he had followed Jesus, he would have been full of joy. When Peter took his own advice and pitied himself (marginal reading, Matthew 16:22), denying his Lord and refusing his cross, he wept bitterly. Satan offers to us a primrose path of our own will and pleasure, but it leads to deepest misery. Jesus offers the cross, a denial of our own will, and a narrow way, and it is the way of ever-increasing and everlasting joy.

God called Enoch to walk with Him, "and Enoch walked with God" (Genesis 5:22,24). God called Enoch to speak on his behalf, putting an unpopular word into his mouth, as He did later with Moses and the child Samuel. Because Enoch was willing to speak the word, God anointed him with the Holy Spirit, making him a prophet of the Most High God. "Enoch," says Jude, "prophesied" (verse 14). This was not easy; what was he saying? "The God whom you think is far off and gone away forever, leaving the earth to go on its own way, *is coming back again!*" "Behold, the Lord cometh with ten thousands of His saints" (verse 14). Enoch did not know the when, but he knew the fact that the Lord was returning to earth; and when He returns, said Enoch, He is going to judge you all and execute judgment upon all you ungodly sinners. It was a very dangerous and most unpopular thing to preach, because in those days the earth was filled with violence. Enoch's faith was an obedient faith without regard to the consequences; his great concern was not, "Is it popular?" but "Is it true?" and "Does God want me to say it?"

Think of Enoch's *faith.* "By *faith* Enoch was *translated*" (Hebrews 11:5), which means that he was raptured, caught up. Do not commit the popular error of thinking that he was caught up because he believed in his own rapture. Many have faith in the doctrine of the rapture, a human believism, produced by fervent speeches and exciting books on prophecy; but this will not produce anything except eventual disappointment. It is faith in *God* that qualifies. Jesus said, "Have faith in God" (Mark 11:22). It was not an *act* of faith, single and alone, that Enoch (and later, Abraham) had, but *an attitude of heart*, believing God all the time.

Abraham believed God as a continual experience, always, about everything. This was the faith that was imputed to him for righteousness, not his believing God for a certain thing on a special occasion. Enoch so believed God that without hesitation, without fear of the consequences to himself, he spoke the Lord's word. He prophesied according to the proportion of faith that he had, which, Paul declares, is the way of truth (Romans 12:6). This is the mark of the true prophet; we wish that there were more such. Today is the day of the pseudo-prophet who by many is considered authentic if he can gush in a string of Bible texts and pleasant promises over simple, genuine, but gullible souls, the rhapsody often being slanted to his own advantage. "The Lord is coming with ten thousands of His saints," said Enoch. This required considerable faith to announce. How many saints had lived from the beginning until then? How many were living when he said it? How many saints did God find to put into the ark? Only eight—and some of these do not seem to have been exceptional characters; one thinks of Ham (Genesis 9:20-24).

Enoch's Character

The *character* of Enoch qualified him for rapture, and this must be our character, too. He walked with God, every day; he did not have a sabbath-day religion. Every step and every action was with one motive—to please God. The present-day equivalent is the admonition, "And whatsoever ye do in word or deed, do all in the name of the Lord Jesus, giving thanks to God the Father by Him" (Colossians 3:17). It must be emphasized that this does not mean that one must tag the name "Jesus" to every action and bring the name "Jesus" into every sentence; but that every word and action must proceed from the indwelling Jesus and be done with one, sole motive—to please God the Father. Only that which is of the Son pleases the Father, and did so in the beginning, ages of ages before ever the human name "Jesus" was adopted by the Logos, when He became incarnate in man, late in time. "This is My beloved Son," said the Father, "in whom I am well pleased" (Matthew 3:17). He ever has been the Father's Beloved, and ever will be. The Father ever has been well pleased with the Son, and ever will be, and we have been adopted "to the praise of the glory of His grace, wherein He hath made us accepted in the Beloved" (Ephesians 1:6).

> *Wherefore God also hath highly exalted Him, and given Him a name which is above every name; that in the name of Jesus every knee should bow, of things in heaven and things in earth, and things under the earth; [11]And that every tongue should confess that Jesus Christ is Lord, to the glory of God the Father.*
>
> *Philippians 2:10-11*

It is in the name of Jesus that every knee shall bow. The Greek preposition is ***en***, translated *at* in the King James Authorized Version of the Bible. The Greek word *en* has a much deeper significance than is given in this translation. It has the sense of "being or remaining *within*, with the primary idea of rest and continuance" (Bullinger).[9] The Holy Spirit is speaking here of a voluntary bowing the knee to the Lordship of the Son. God is not interested in compelling the bowing of the knees of rebels when their hearts are still alien to Him; that would be but a manifestation of His ability to crush opposition. Impenitent rebels who have refused Christ will have their part in the lake of fire.

Paul says: "I give you to understand... that no man can say that Jesus is the Lord but by the Holy Ghost" (1 Corinthians

12:3); the only lauding of the Son that the Father desires from humanity is a glad and voluntary acknowledgment of His Lordship, in love rising from the heart. This alone, coming from those who once were rebels, aliens, and strangers, but who are now reconciled to God through the blood of His Son, gives glory to God the Father.

The most amazing miracle and manifestation of divine grace that ever has been or could be was the Incarnation, which was the gift by the Father of His Son, and the Son's voluntary descent to the earth that He had once created, becoming visible in the actual person of a man. This was not a *theophany* (that is, God assuming merely the *appearance* of a human being, as He did, for example, to Abraham),[10] but a real and literal putting on of human nature in its completeness of body, soul, and spirit. When He did this, He took a common and familiar Jewish name, *Yeshua* (Joshua), known more familiarly to us in its Greek form of *Jesus*; then, ascending to the Father after His resurrection, He ascended as the Divine-man—God forever compounded with the humanity that He had glorified. He was the first man to enter into the true Holy of Holies, the presence of the Father, so that He was the leader of many who, like Him, should be conceived and born of the Holy Spirit and brought as sons into the Glory. No man, not even Enoch or Elijah, had entered that holy place, the immediate presence of God; for as Jesus said, "No man hath ascended up to [the] Heaven" (John 3:13). Enoch and Elijah had been taken up into the *heavens* and then had waited with all of the other saints in Paradise, in *Sheol* (Greek: *Hades*), until the coming of the Deliverer. After the resurrection and ascension of our Lord, a new name was known in Heaven. The Logos, the Eternal One, Son of the Father, had glorified the name Jesus, and all the angels of God bowed low before a human name.

At the name of Jesus
Every knee shall bow,
Every tongue confess Him
King of glory now:
'Tis the Father's pleasure
We should call Him Lord,
Who from the beginning
Was the mighty Word.

At His voice, creation
Sprang at once to sight—
All the angel faces,
All the hosts of light,
Thrones and dominations,
Stars upon their way,
All the heavenly orders,
In their great array.

Humbled for a season,
To receive a Name
From the lips of sinners
Unto whom He came;
Faithfully He bore it,
Spotless to the last,
Brought it back victorious,
When from death He passed.

Bore it up triumphant
With its human light
Through all ranks of creatures,
To the central height,
To the throne of Godhead,
To the Father's breast;
Filled it with the glory
Of that perfect rest.[11]

—Caroline M. Noel—

Enoch's Testimony

Enoch had a good testimony—"for before his translation, he had this testimony, that he pleased God" (Hebrews 11:5). That is the only kind of testimony that is worth anything—one that pleases God. If Enoch had been running a used car lot, his utter truthfulness about the models he was showing would have pleased God. If Enoch had been a lawyer, his selfless interest in justice and in the welfare of the innocent would have pleased God. If Enoch had been an employer of labor, his payment of a fair day's pay for an honest day's work, and his deep interest and concern for the good of his workers and their families would have pleased God. If Enoch had been an employee, his honest day's work and freedom from pilfering his employer's property would have pleased God—and so on. This is the practical overcoming life that *before* rapture (note very specially this word *before*) qualifies the Christian for it. All arguments that justify sin in the Christian are against Scripture and are the product of the carnal mind. The Bible agrees with the doctrine of the final perseverance of *saints*, but knows nothing about a doctrine of the final perseverance of *sinners*. Enoch did what Adam had once done in Eden: he walked and talked with God. Amos tells us that "two cannot walk together unless they are agreed" (Amos 3:3). Enoch agreed with God about everything; his attitude was "not my will but thine be done." He agreed with God in holiness; he agreed with God in truth. He had the character of God, which is godliness; how indignant he was with ungodliness. He said that God was coming "to execute judgment upon all, and to convince all that are *ungodly* among them of all their *ungodly* deeds which they have *ungodly* committed and of all their hard speeches which *ungodly* sinners have spoken against Him" (Jude 15). For Enoch loved God, and to those who love God, all thought and action contrary to Him is utterly abhorrent.

Enoch's Triumph: The Final Triumph of Faith

So Enoch triumphed—"he was not... for God took him" (Genesis 5:24). He was caught up, seen no more on the earth. He vanished. He disappeared. He became one of the waiting saints, one of the tens of thousands who, coming with their Lord, will welcome the New Covenant Enochs, those fully consecrated to God like him, who in that Great Day will join the Lord and all that holy company in the air.

When the Lord spoke of His return and emphasized that the condition of the times would be just as they were in the days of Noah, He made it clear that there would be division. The first division would be between the righteous and the wicked. The wicked would continue in their carelessness and sinning as they did in antediluvian[12] times "until the day Noah entered into the ark... and the flood came and took them all away" (Matthew 24:37-39).

The Lord then reveals a second division. He proceeds to say, "Then shall two be in the field; the one shall be taken and the other left," and so with the two grinding at the mill and the two asleep in bed. To whom is He speaking? He is speaking to His disciples, for He says, "Watch therefore, for ye know not what hour your Lord doth come" (Matthew 24:42). If there is no difference between the watchful and the unwatchful, then why does He give such a constant and insistent repetition of the call to watch? It is confirmed in the parable of the wise and unwise virgins (Matthew 25:1-13). They are all virgins. The Lord calls none but His own *virgins*; the unregenerate are not called virgins by the Lord Jesus Christ. The watching virgins go in to the Bridegroom's house, to a prolonged time of feasting, for that was the marriage custom when the Lord was upon the earth. The unwise virgins are not shut out into outer darkness; but neither are they brought in to the marriage feast, which is the "marriage supper of the Lamb."

Again, the Lord concludes with the solemn warning, "Watch therefore!" Why were the foolish virgins not invited in? It was not because they did not have a reserve of oil, but because they were not watching. If their minds had been set to watch until He came, they would have made provision for it by having a reserve vessel of oil. This is equivalent to our trusting the Lord to continue to renew us with ever-successive infillings of the Holy Spirit, rising up in overflowing measure from that well of living water, the abiding Holy Spirit within. *This alone enables the lover of Jesus to watch with and for Him.* The wise virgins are the Enochs of the latter days, and, in another figure, they are the firstfruits of the wheat harvest that the Son of God shall reap. (See Revelation 14, especially verse 4.) All of the wheat represents His own; but the firstfruits are gathered before the general harvest. In the days of the Old Covenant, God ordained that, before the harvest was gathered, "ye shall bring a sheaf of the firstfruits of your harvest unto the priest; and he shall wave the sheaf before the LORD" (Leviticus 23:9-11). The first ripe, the very best, was lifted up to the Lord, typifying the bridal saints, the ones who are the undefiled virgins "which follow the Lamb whithersoever He goeth.... In their mouth was found no guile: for they are without fault before the throne of God." These are "the firstfruits unto God and to the Lamb" (Revelation 14:4-5). After these are caught up, there follows the general harvest, gathered with a sharp sickle by the Son of Man crowned with a golden crown (verses 14-16).

The same truth is given in another figure in Revelation 12—a woman clothed with the sun, with the moon under her feet, crowned with stars, is delivered of a "man child, who is to rule all nations with a rod of iron," and is "caught up unto God, and to His throne." Whatever other interpretations of these scriptures there may be, they enshrine the same principle of a selection from the selection. Some are caught away from tribulation to come, while others are saved by passing through tribulation, like the woman who was "given two wings of a great eagle, that she could fly into the wilderness" from the wrath of the dragon, and be there preserved by God. This truth is made unequivocally clear by the Lord Jesus who said, "Watch ye therefore, and pray always, that ye may be accounted worthy to escape all these things that shall come to pass, and to stand before the Son of Man" (Luke 21:36).

So Enoch "was not found, for God had translated him," which means that they looked for him but could not find him. Who looked for him? Not the people of the world, but the people of God. Who looked for Elijah when he was raptured? Not the king of Israel, nor his corrupt court, nor the people he reigned over, but the "sons of the prophets" (2 Kings 2:16-18). Who will look for the Enochs raptured before the tribulation of God's judgments upon the earth? It will not be the people of this world, but the people of God, the Noahs, the Shems, the Hams, the Japheths, and the sons of the prophets. The highly seasoned, journalistic accounts of the frantic concern of the populace at the sudden disappearance of the saints at the second coming of the Lord Jesus exist only in imagination. It is of the category of fiction. There is no suggestion of any such panic mentioned anywhere in the Bible.

This is the final triumph of faith—to be raptured, to be forever with the Lord, to share His millennial reign. The Lord's steward had watched in diligence and was found faithful. But what of those saints who have already passed on and who were in Christ, *really* in Christ, not in word only, but in deed and in truth, who before their decease walked with God in holiness? What has the Scripture to say of these? It says, "Blessed and holy is he that hath part in the first resurrection... they shall be priests of God and of Christ, and shall reign with Him a thousand years" (Revelation 20:6). God makes a difference between the holy and the righteous, as He does between the unjust and the filthy; for the time is shortly coming when it will be too late to qualify, and the Lord will say, "He that is righteous, let him be righteous still: and he that is holy, let him be holy still" (Revelation 22:11). When Paul was on earth, he longed that he might qualify for this first resurrection:

> *That I may know Him, and the power of His resurrection and the fellowship of His sufferings, being conformed to His death; [11]in order that I may attain to the resurrection from the dead. [12]Not that I have already obtained it, or have already become perfect, but I press on... [14]I press on toward the goal for the prize of the upward call of God in Christ Jesus. [15]Let us therefore, as many as are perfect, have this attitude.*
>
> *Philippians 3:10-12,14-15* NASB

Here we say farewell, with a word of loving advice. Even if you are unconvinced of the truth of this final triumph of faith and its glorious reward, will you nevertheless ask for constant grace that you may be like Enoch for Jesus' sake? Jesus loves you with an everlasting love. He has drawn you to Himself. Then, without a thought for the gift of a celestial crown or even of reward for the faithful, but just because He is your Beloved, live so as to please Him, for "in such an hour as ye think not, the Son of man cometh" (Matthew 24:44).

Then the end: Thy Church completed,
All Thy chosen gathered in,
With their King in glory seated,
Satan bound, and banished sin;
Gone forever parting, weeping,
Hunger, sorrow, death, and pain.

Lo! her watch Thy Church is keeping;
Come, Lord Jesus, come to reign![13]

—Henry Downton—

Amen!

ENDNOTES FOR CHAPTER 10

1. *Start,* in this context, is what structural parts do when they *work loose from position or fastening.*

2. The allusion is to the enemy army in the story of Gideon (Judges 6-7).

3. *Methuselah* means *when he is dead it* [the Flood] *shall be sent.* See *The Exhaustive Dictionary of Bible Names* by Judson Cornwall and Stelman Smith (North Brunswick, NJ: Bridge-Logos), p. 173.

4. Pastor Gutteridge brings out the word actually used by Peter in the Greek text. The words normally translated as *hell* in the New Testament are either ***Hades*** (the place of the departed dead awaiting judgment) or ***Gehenna*** (the place of eternal punishment). In 2 Peter 2:4 only, we encounter the Greek verb *tartaro,* which means literally "to cast into ***Tartarus.***" In the understanding of ancient (non-biblical) Greek writers, Tartarus was the place into which the ancient race of the Titans had been cast and imprisoned by the Olympian gods. Though it seems strange at first glance that Peter would employ a place-name taken from Greek mythology, his word choice was consistent with the Septuagint (LXX), that is, the Greek translation of the Old Testament available in his day. In that translation, the phrase "valley of the Rephaim" is rendered "valley of the *Titans*" in 2 Samuel 5:18,22. A similar translation is also found in at least one other passage, this one from the Apocrypha (Judith 16:7), where reference is made to "the sons of the *Titans.*" Peter undoubtedly discerned the echo of truth in the ancient Greek stories regarding God's punishment of these fallen angels.

5. In his booklet, *The Black Hole* (FinestOfTheWheat.org/blackhole-all), Pastor Gutteridge considered the imprisonment of these fallen angels from a unique perspective.

---

6. *Noachian:* of or relating to the patriarch Noah
7. Flavius Josephus (37-100 A.D.), born Joseph ben Matthias, was a Jewish eyewitness of the Roman siege and destruction of Jerusalem in 70 A.D. His account can be found in his *Wars of the Jews*, Books 4-7.
8. From the poem *Along the Road*
9. The quote is from Ethelbert William Bullinger's copiously annotated work, *The Companion Bible.* The note on Philippians 2:10 about the preposition "at" (page 1776) refers the reader to Appendix 104, item 8 ("viii"), where the quote Pastor Gutteridge uses is to be found (appendix page 149). Pastor Gutteridge frequently recommended *The Companion Bible.*
10. As in Genesis 18. The subject of theophanies is pursued further in a Kernels of Wheat Bible Study entitled *Who Was the Angel of the LORD?* (FinestOfTheWheat.org/kindle-aotl)
11. For the hymn ***At the Name of Jesus***, see page 200 in the appendix.
12. *Antediluvian:* of or relating to the period before the Flood related in Genesis 6-8
13. This is the last verse of ***Lord, Her Watch Thy Church Is Keeping*** (full text in the appendix on page 202).

Appendix: Hymns of the Faith

Appendix of Hymns

Anyone who loved to hear Percy Gutteridge minister will remember his frequent and inspired use of poetry in his messages, especially from the vast treasury of the Church's hymns of the faith. As we have worked with Pastor's material over the last twenty years, whether written works, audio files, or transcripts, we have been amazed at his memory and mastery of "the songs of Zion." Equally impressive, in retrospect, was his special gift of being able to impart the value of and his love for these classics to his hearers. (What else can explain how a church of young "Jesus people" wound up making the *Redemption Hymnal* its primary songbook?)

In a day when hymnals, and perhaps even deeply devotional, reverential public worship itself, are becoming endangered species, it seemed fitting to append to this third edition of ***Faith Is Substance*** the complete text of the hymns from which Pastor Gutteridge quoted in the preceding chapters. We present them in the same order in which he referred to them in the book, with a hope that they will be read reflectively, sung lovingly, and enjoyed worshipfully. May they serve the same purpose to which Pastor would have employed them during his lifetime—to sweetly and powerfully emphasize and enhance the truth Percy Gutteridge was called to preach, and to introduce a new generation to the incomparable riches of the inspired poets of Christendom.

Jim & Denise Kerwin
February 2019

O Love Divine, How Sweet Thou Art!

Charles Wesley

1707-1788

(Quoted on page 4)

O love divine, how sweet thou art!
When shall I find my willing heart
All taken up by Thee?
I thirst, I faint, I die to prove
The greatness of redeeming love,
The love of Christ to me.

Stronger His love than death or hell;
Its riches are unsearchable.
The first-born sons of light
Desire in vain its depths to see;
They cannot reach the mystery,
The length, and breadth, and height.

God only knows the love of God;
O that it now were shed abroad
In this poor stony heart!
For love I sigh, for love I pine;
This only portion, Lord, be mine,
Be mine this better part!

O that I could forever sit
With Mary at the Master's feet!
Be this my happy choice,
My only care, delight, and bliss,
My joy, my heaven on earth, be this —
To hear the Bridegroom's voice!

O that, with humbled Peter, I
Could weep, believe, and thrice reply,
My faithfulness to prove.
Thou know'st, (for all to Thee is known),
Thou know'st, O Lord, and Thou alone,
Thou know'st that Thee I love.

O that I could, with favored John,
Recline my weary head upon
The dear Redeemer's breast!
From care, and sin, and sorrow free,
Give me, O Lord, to find in Thee
My everlasting rest.

The Galilean Fishers Toil

Christopher Wordsworth
1807-1885
(Quoted on page 7)

The Galilean fishers toil
All night and nothing take;
But Jesus comes—a wondrous spoil
Is lifted from the lake.
Lord, when our labours are in vain,
And vain the help of men,
When fruitless is our care and pain—
Come blessèd Jesus then!

The night is dark, the surges fill
The bark, the wild winds roar;
But Jesus comes, and all is still—
The ship is at the shore.
O Lord, when storms around us howl,
And all is dark and drear,
In all the tempests of the soul,
O blessèd Jesus, hear!

A frail one, thrice denying Thee,
Saw mercy in Thine eyes;
The penitent upon the tree
Was borne to paradise.
In hours of sin and deep distress,
O show us, Lord, Thy face;
In penitential loneliness,
O give us, Jesus, grace!

The faithful few retire in fear
To their closed upper room,
But suddenly, with joyful cheer,
They see their Master come.
Lord, come to us, unloose our bands
And bid our terrors cease;
Lift over us Thy blessèd hands,
Speak, holy Jesus, peace.

Spirit of Faith, Come Down

Charles Wesley

1707-1788

(Quoted on page 11)

Spirit of faith, come down,
Reveal the things of God,
And make to us the Godhead known,
And witness with the blood.
'Tis Thine the blood to apply,
And give us eyes to see;
Who did for every sinner die
Hath surely died for me.

No man can truly say
That Jesus is the Lord
Unless Thou take the veil away
And breathe the living word:
Then, only then we feel
Our interest in the blood,
And cry with joy unspeakable,
"Thou art my Lord, my God!"

I know my Saviour lives;
He lives, who died for me.
My inmost soul His voice receives
Who hangs on yonder tree:
Set forth before my eyes,
E'en now I see him bleed,
And hear His mortal groans, and cries,
While suffering in my stead.

O that the world may know
The great, atoning Lamb!
Spirit of Faith, descend and show
The virtue of His name;
The grace which all may find,
The saving power impart,
And testify to all mankind,
And speak to every heart.

Inspire the living faith,
Which whosoe'er receives
The witness in himself he hath,
And consciously believes;
The faith that conquers all,
And doth the mountains move,
And saves whoe'er on Jesus call,
And perfects them in love.

Through All the Changing Scenes of Life

Nahum Tate & Nicholas Brady

(Quoted on page 32)

Through all the changing scenes of life,
In trouble and in joy,
The praises of my God shall still
My heart and tongue employ.

Of His deliverance I will boast,
Till all that are distressed
From my example courage take
And soothe their griefs to rest.

O magnify the Lord with me,
With me exalt His name;
When in distress to Him I called,
He to my rescue came.

Their drooping hearts were soon refreshed,
Who looked to Him for aid,
Desired success in every face,
A cheerful air displayed.

"Behold," they say, "Behold the man
Whom Providence relieved;
The man so dangerously beset,
So wondrously retrieved!"

The hosts of God encamp around
The dwellings of the just;
Deliv'rance He affords to all
Who on His succour trust.

O make but trial of His love;
Experience will decide
How blest are they, and only they,
Who in His truth confide.

Fear Him, ye saints, and you will then
Have nothing else to fear.
Make you His service your delight;
Your want shall be His care.

While hungry lions lack their prey,
The Lord will food provide
For such as put their trust in Him,
And see their needs supplied.

Blest Are the Humble Souls That See

Isaac Watts

(Quoted on 40)

The Beatitudes (Matthew 5:2-12) set to verse

Blest are the humble souls that see
Their emptiness and poverty;
Treasures of grace to them are giv'n,
And crowns of joy laid up in heav'n.

Blest are the men of broken heart,
Who mourn for sin with inward smart;
The blood of Christ divinely flows,
A healing balm for all their woes.

Blest are the meek, who stand afar
From rage and passion, noise and war;
God will secure their happy state,
And plead their cause against the great.

Blest are the souls that thirst for grace,
Hunger and long for righteousness;
They shall be well supplied, and fed
With living streams and living bread.

Blest are the men whose bowels move
And melt with sympathy and love;
From Christ the Lord shall they obtain
Like sympathy and love again.

Blest are the pure, whose hearts are clean
From the defiling pow'r of sin;
With endless pleasure they shall see
A God of spotless purity.

Blest are the men of peaceful life,
Who quench the coals of growing strife;
They shall be called the heirs of bliss,
The sons of God, the God of peace.

Blest are the suff'rers who partake
Of pain and shame for Jesus' sake.
Their souls shall triumph in the Lord;
Glory and joy are their reward.

Father of Jesus Christ, My Lord

Charles Wesley

(Quoted on page 41)

Romans 4:13ff

Father of Jesus Christ, my Lord,
My Saviour, and my Head,
I trust in Thee, whose powerful word
Hath raised Him from the dead.

Thou know'st for my offence He died,
And rose again for me,
Fully and freely justified,
That I might live to Thee.

Eternal life to all mankind
Thou hast in Jesus given;
And all who seek, in Him shall find
The happiness of heaven.

O God! Thy record I believe,
In Abraham's footsteps tread;
And wait, expecting to receive
The Christ, the Promised Seed.

Faith in Thy power Thou seest I have,
For Thou this faith hast wrought;
Dead souls Thou callest from their grave,
And speakest worlds from nought.

Things that are not, as though they were,
Thou callest by their name;
Present and future with Thee are,
With Thee, the great I AM.

In hope, against all human hope,
Self-desperate, I believe;
Thy quickening word shall raise me up,
Thou shalt Thy Spirit give.

The thing surpasses all my thought,
But faithful is my Lord;
Through unbelief I stagger not,
For God hath spoke the word.

Faith, mighty faith, the promise sees,
And looks to that alone,
Laughs at impossibilities,
And cries, "It shall be done!"

To Thee the glory of Thy power
And faithfulness I give;
I shall in Christ, in that glad hour,
And Christ in me shall live.

Obedient faith, that waits on Thee,
Thou never wilt reprove;
But thou wilt form Thy Son in me,
And perfect me in love.

Be Thou Removed

Joseph Ellison

(Quoted on page 55)

When mountain walls confront thy way,
Why sit and weep? Arise and say,
"Be thou removed!" and they shall be,
By power of God, cast in the sea.

All power on earth, all power in heaven
To Christ, the Son of God, is given;
And from the throne He will endue,
And hindrances shall flee from you.

O'er all the power of fiend or man,
Say to the Lord, "I surely can!"
Take from Him power on earth to tread
On serpent's sting, on dragon's head.

Whate'er thou art, O mountain high,
Where'er thou art, in earth or sky,
Whene'er thou art, truth is the same,
"Be thou removed, in Jesus' name!"

"Be thou removed!" Faith bids thee start
For yonder sea–Arise! Depart!
I may, I can, I must, I will
The purpose of my God fulfill.

O Thou Who Camest from Above

Charles Wesley

(Quoted on page 62)

O Thou who camest from above,
The pure celestial fire t' impart,
Kindle a flame of sacred love
On the mean altar of my heart.

There let it for Thy glory burn
With inextinguishable blaze,
And trembling to its source return,
In humble prayer and fervent praise.

Jesus, confirm my heart's desire
To work and speak and think for Thee;
Still let me guard the holy fire,
And still stir up Thy gift in me.

Ready for all Thy perfect will,
My acts of faith and love repeat,
Till death Thy endless mercies seal,
And make my sacrifice complete.

I Want a Principle Within

Charles Wesley

(Quoted on page 68)

I want a principle within
Of watchful, godly fear,
A sensibility of sin,
A pain to feel it near.
I want the first approach to feel
Of pride or wrong desire,
To catch the wand'ring of my will,
And quench the kindling fire.

From Thee that I no more may stray,
No more Thy goodness grieve,
Grant me the filial awe, I pray,
The tender conscience give.
Quick as the apple of an eye,
O God, my conscience make;
Awake my soul when sin is nigh,
And keep it still awake.

Almighty God of truth and love,
To me Thy power impart;
The mountain from my soul remove,
The hardness from my heart.
O may the least omission pain
My reawakened soul,
And drive me to that blood again,
Which makes the wounded whole.

Blessèd Lord, in Thee Is Refuge

Herbert Booth

(Quoted on page 77)

Blessèd Lord, in Thee is refuge,
Safety for my trembling soul,
Pow'r to lift my head when drooping
'Midst the angry billows' roll.
I will trust Thee; all my life Thou shalt control.

In the past, too unbelieving
'Midst the tempest I have been,
And my heart has slowly trusted
What my eyes have never seen.
Blessèd Jesus, teach me on Thine arm to lean.

O, for trust that brings the triumph
When defeat seems strangely near;
O, for faith that changes fighting
Into vict'ry's ringing cheer!
Faith triumphant, knowing not defeat nor fear.

Faith triumphant—blessèd vict'ry!
Every barrier swept away,
Heaven descending, joy and fullness,
Dawn of everlasting day!
Jesus only, Him to love and Him obey.

They Who Know the Saviour

Mrs. C.H. Morris

(Quoted on page 83)

They who know the Saviour shall in Him be strong,
Mighty in the conflict of the right 'gainst wrong.
This the blessèd promise given in God's Word,
Doing wondrous exploits, they who know the Lord.

Chorus:
Victory! victory! blessèd blood-bought victory,
Victory! victory! vict'ry all the time;
As Jehovah liveth, strength divine He giveth
Unto those who know Him, vict'ry all the time.

In the midst of battle be not thou dismayed,
Tho' the powers of darkness 'gainst thee are arrayed.
God, thy strength, is with thee, causing thee to stand;
Heaven's allied armies wait at thy command.

Brave to bear life's testing, strong the foe to meet,
Walking like a hero midst the furnace heat,
Doing wondrous exploits with the Spirit's sword,
Winning souls for Jesus—praise, O praise the Lord!

All Things Are Possible to Him

Charles Wesley

(Quoted on page 91)

All things are possible to him
That can in Jesu's name believe;
Lord, I no more Thy truth blaspheme,
Thy truth I lovingly receive;
I can, I do believe in Thee,
All things are possible to me.

The most impossible of all
Is that I e'er from sin should cease;
Yet shall it be: I know it shall;
Jesus, look to Thy faithfulness!
If nothing is too hard for Thee,
All things are possible to me.

Though earth and hell the word gainsay,
The word of God can never fail:
The Lamb shall take my sins away—
'Tis certain though impossible!
The thing impossible shall be:
All things are possible to me.

When Thou the work of faith hast wrought,
I here shall in Thine image shine,
Nor sin in deed or word or thought.
Let men exclaim, and fiends repine;
They cannot break the firm decree:
All things are possible to me.

The unchangeable decree is past,
The sure, predestinating word
That I, who on my Lord am cast,
I shall be like my sinless Lord;
'Twas fixed from all eternity:
All things are possible to me.

Thy mouth, O Lord, hath spoke, hath sworn
That I shall serve Thee without fear,
Shall find the pearl which others spurn,
Holy, and pure, and perfect here.
The servant as his Lord shall be:
All things are possible to me.

All things are possible to God,
To Christ the power of God in man,
To me, when I am all renewed,
When I in Christ am born again,
And witness, from all sin set free:
All things are possible to me!

Church of God, Beloved and Chosen

Frances Ridley Havergal

(Quoted on page 93)

Church of God, beloved and chosen,
Church of Christ, for whom He died,
Claim thy gifts and praise the Giver.
"Ye are washed and sanctified,"
Sanctified by God the Father,
And by Jesus Christ His Son,

And by God, the Holy Spirit,
Holy, Holy, Three in One.

By His will He sanctifieth,
By the Spirit's power within,
By the loving hand that chasteneth,
Fruits of righteousness to win;
By His truth and by His promise,
By the Word, His gift unpriced,
By His own blood, and by union
With the risen life of Christ.

Holiness by faith in Jesus,
Not by effort of thine own;
Sin's dominion crushed and broken
By the power of grace alone.
God's own holiness within thee,
His own beauty on thy brow:
This shall be thy pilgrim brightness,
This thy blessèd portion now.

He will sanctify thee wholly;
Body, spirit, soul shall be
Blameless till thy Saviour's coming
In His glorious majesty!
He hath perfected forever
Those whom He hath sanctified;
Spotless, glorious, and holy
Is the church, His chosen Bride.

Wrestling Jacob

Charles Wesley

(Quoted on page 106)

Come, O Thou Traveller unknown,
Whom still I hold, but cannot see;
My company before is gone,
And I am left alone with Thee.
With Thee all night I mean to stay
And wrestle till the break of day.

I need not tell Thee who I am,
My misery, or sin, declare;
Thyself hast call'd me by my Name,
Look on Thy hand and read it there.
But who, I ask Thee, who art Thou?
Tell me Thy name, and tell me now!

In vain Thou strugglest to get free,
I never will unloose my hold;
Art Thou the Man that died for me?
The secret of Thy love unfold;
Wrestling I will not let Thee go,
Till I Thy name, Thy nature know.

Wilt Thou not yet to me reveal
Thy new, unutterable name?
Tell me, I still beseech Thee, tell,
To know it now resolv'd I am;
Wrestling I will not let Thee go
Till I Thy name, Thy nature know.

'Tis all in vain to hold Thy tongue,
Or touch the hollow of my thigh;
Though every sinew be unstrung,
Out of my arms Thou shalt not fly.
Wrestling I will not let Thee go,
Till I Thy name, Thy nature know.

What tho' my shrinking flesh complain,
And murmur to contend so long,
I rise superior to my pain;
When I am weak then I am strong.
And when my all of strength shall fail,
I shall with the God-man prevail.

My strength is gone, my nature dies,
I sink beneath Thy weighty hand,
Faint to revive, and fall to rise;
I fall, and yet by faith I stand,
I stand, and will not let Thee go,
Till I Thy name, Thy nature know.

Yield to me now—for I am weak,
But confident in self-despair;
Speak to my heart, in blessing speak,
Be conquer'd by my instant prayer;
Speak, or Thou never hence shalt move,
And tell me if Thy name is Love.

'Tis Love, 'tis Love! Thou diedst for Me,
I hear Thy whisper in my heart.
The morning breaks, the shadows flee:
Pure universal Love Thou art;

To me, to all, Thy mercies move –
Thy nature, and Thy name is Love.

My prayer hath power with God; the grace
unspeakable I now receive;
Thro' faith I see Thee face to face,
I see Thee face to face, and live:
In vain I have not wept, and strove,
Thy nature, and Thy name is Love.

I know Thee, Saviour, who Thou art,
Jesus, the feeble sinner's friend;
Nor wilt Thou with the night depart,
But stay, and love me to the end;
Thy mercies never shall remove,
Thy nature, and Thy name is Love.

The Sun of Righteousness on me
Hath ris'n with healing in His wings,
With'ring my nature's strength; from Thee
My Soul its life and succour brings,
My help is all laid up above;
Thy nature and Thy name is Love.

Contented now upon my thigh
I halt, till life's short journey end;
All helplessness, all weakness I,
On Thee alone for strength depend,
Nor have I power from Thee to move;
Thy nature, and Thy name is Love.

Lame as I am, I take the prey,
Hell, earth, and sin with ease o'ercome;
I leap for joy, pursue my way,
And as a bounding hart fly home,
Through all eternity to prove
Thy nature and Thy name is Love.

God Moves in a Mysterious Way

William Cowper

(Quoted on page 112)

God moves in a mysterious way
His wonders to perform;
He plants His footsteps in the sea
And rides upon the storm.

Deep in unfathomable mines
Of never-failing skill,
He treasures up His bright designs
And works His sovereign will.

Ye fearful saints, fresh courage take;
The clouds ye so much dread
Are big with mercy, and shall break
In blessings on your head.

Judge not the Lord by feeble sense,
But trust Him for His grace;
Behind a frowning providence
He hides a smiling face.

His purposes will ripen fast,
Unfolding every hour;
The bud may have a bitter taste,
But sweet will be the flower.

Blind unbelief is sure to err
And scan His work in vain;
God is His own interpreter,
And He will make it plain.

Infinite, Unexhausted Love

Charles Wesley

(Quoted on page 135)

Infinite, unexhausted Love!
Jesus and love are one!
If still to me Thy mercies move,
They are restrained to none.

What shall I do, my God to love,
My loving God to praise?
The length, and breadth, and height to prove,
And depth of sovereign grace?

Thy sovereign grace to all extends,
Immense and unconfined;
From age to age it never ends—
It reaches all mankind.

Throughout the world its breadth is known,
Wide as infinity;
So wide it never passed by one,
Or it had passed by me.

My trespass was grown up to heav'n;
But far above the skies,
In Christ abundantly forgiven,
I see Thy mercies rise.

The depth of all-redeeming love
What angel-tongue can tell?
O may I to the utmost prove
The gift unspeakable!

Deeper than hell, it plucked me thence;
Deeper than inbred sin,
Jesus's love my heart shall cleanse
When Jesus enters in.

Come quickly, gracious Lord, and take
Possession of Thine own;
My longing heart vouchsafe to make
Thine everlasting throne!

Assert Thy claim, receive Thy right,
Come quickly from above,
And sink me to perfection's height,
The depth of humble love.

At the Name of Jesus

Caroline M. Noel

(Quoted on page 166)

At the name of Jesus every knee shall bow,
Every tongue confess Him King of Glory now;
'Tis the Father's pleasure we should call Him Lord,
Who from the beginning was the mighty Word.

Mighty and mysterious in the highest height,
God from everlasting, very Light of light;
In the Father's bosom, with the Spirit blest,
Love, in Love eternal, Rest, in perfect rest.

At His voice, creation sprang at once to sight,
All the angel faces, all the hosts of light,
Thrones and dominations, stars upon their way,
All the heavenly orders in their great array.

Humbled for a season to receive a name
From the lips of sinners unto whom He came,
Faithfully He bore it, spotless to the last,
Brought it back victorious when from death He passed.

Bore it up triumphant with its human light
Through all ranks of creatures to the central height,
To the throne of Godhead, to the Father's breast;
Filled it with the glory of that perfect rest.

Name Him, brothers, name Him, with love strong as death,
But with awe and wonder, and with bated breath!
He is God the Saviour, He is Christ the Lord,
Ever to be worshipped, trusted, and adored.

In your hearts enthrone Him; there let Him subdue
All that is not holy, all that is not true;
Crown Him as your Captain in temptation's hour;
Let His will enfold you in its light and power.

Brothers, this Lord Jesus shall return again
With His Father's glory, with His angel train;
For all wreaths of empire meet upon His brow,
And our hearts confess Him King of Glory now.

Lord, Her Watch Thy Church Is Keeping

Henry Downton

(Quoted on page 171)

Lord, her watch Thy Church is keeping;
When shall earth Thy rule obey?
When shall end the night of weeping?
When shall break the promised day?
See the whitening harvest languish,
Waiting still the laborers' toil;
Was it vain, Thy Son's deep anguish?
Shall the strong retain the spoil?

Tidings, sent to every creature,
Millions yet have never heard;
Can they hear without a preacher?
Lord almighty, give the word!
Give the word! In every nation
Let the Gospel trumpet sound,
Witnessing a world's salvation,
To the earth's remotest bound.

Then the end! Thy Church completed,
All Thy chosen gathered in,
With their King in glory seated,
Satan bound, and banished sin,
Gone forever parting, weeping,
Hunger, sorrow, death, and pain.
Lo! her watch Thy Church is keeping;
Come, Lord Jesus, come to reign!

Notes
about the Book
and the Author

Editors' Notes

IN THE FORTY-FOUR YEARS since the original publication of ***Faith Is Substance*** in 1975, we have not encountered another book remotely similar to it. Its wisdom and counsel and insight come from a lifetime of the author's walk in the Spirit—by faith. The "validity and vitality" of the book's message, as Dr. Frost rightly observed in the original foreword, flows from the fact that its truths grew out of "the crucible of experience" in the life of its author, Rev. Percy Herbert Paul Gutteridge.

The book is unique because P. H. P. Gutteridge was one of a kind. Besides being a dear father in the Lord to us, imparting God's truth and wisdom with such foundational influence in our lives, Percy was beloved by many as a pastor, and even more highly regarded as a Spirit-filled Teacher (we capitalize the word in the sense of Ephesians 4:11) of God's Word. The Lord has laid it on our hearts that Percy's vital insights and teachings should continue to be made available to the Church today. Because the vision of keeping Pastor Gutteridge's ministry alive is in our hearts, and since his book has been out of print for over three decades, the undertaking of editing and republishing ***Faith Is Substance*** in print was all but inevitable.

Although editing is part of the process of reissuing any book, we have approached the process with utmost care and humility, keeping foremost in mind that we want the republished book to remain in every aspect Percy's words and intent. Over the years, the kind responses to the book's content on the

FinestOfTheWheat.org

website have confirmed that we have succeeded in making enhancements without diminishing the "classic Percy" style and focus. With this in mind, we summarize here our editorial contributions and emendations:

- *Paragraph breaks:* Longer paragraphs (some one to two pages in length) were broken into smaller paragraphs, following the conventions most modern readers expect.

- *Headings:* Section headings and subheadings were added throughout, to organizationally assist the 21st-Century reader with the flow of the material, and in some places key points were bulleted.

- *Typeface:* We have employed a larger, updated type style.

- *Scripture references:* Usually, but not always, Pastor added in parentheses the Bible references for the verses he quoted or to which he referred. We have taken the liberty of adding many Scripture references where omitted.

- *Endnotes:* Endnotes have been added to the chapters. Their aim is to clarify unusual terms, to aid the reader with brief historical backgrounds, or to establish the name and author of a work from which Pastor Gutteridge quotes. The notes are sequestered away at each chapter's end and may be ignored or perused at the discretion of the reader.

- *Appendix of Hymns:* In the text Percy draws from many of his beloved hymns of the faith, so we felt led by the Lord to add to *Faith Is Substance* an appendix of hymns. (See page 177.) When Pastor Gutteridge quotes from a hymn, an endnote details the hymn's name and author, and refers the reader to the appropriate appendix page where the full text of the lyrics can be found. To complete the circle, each hymn in the appendix refers back to the page on which Pastor makes the quote. It is our hope that these "songs of Zion" will be a devotional blessing to the reader, imparting even more of the poetical unction with which Percy Gutteridge's messages were freighted.

- *Clarification:* The few changes to Pastor Gutteridge's wording are minor, and then only for the purpose of clarification.

We believe that this new edition comes forth in a format that is both faithful to the original, and enhanced in such a way as to make it more easily readable—in short, as close as we can make it to the publishing ideal the author appreciated so much.

Respectfully and lovingly submitted,

Jim and Denise Kerwin
February 2019

About the Author

I AM TEMPTED TO MIMIC THE TEXT of John 1:6 and write of the Rev. P.H.P. ("Percy") Gutteridge (1909-1998), "There was a teacher sent from God whose name was Percy Gutteridge." Scripturally, it is true that such teachers are gifts of the Lord Jesus to His Church (Ephesians 4:11). To anyone who sat under Pastor Gutteridge's teaching and preaching, especially during the last thirty years of his long and productive life, his enlightening influence was immeasurable.

His was the gift of inspired, intelligent, deeply spiritual, and yet simple unfolding of the deep truths of God from the Holy Scriptures. To use his own words (though I never recall him using the phrase about himself), he was full of "Holy Ghost common sense"—something which is by no means *common* nowadays! By his private, personal example and in his public ministry, he always pointed to Christ Jesus, ministered His Person, and challenged his listeners to Christ-likeness.

A brief timeline of Pastor's life, written by his son John and daughter-in-law, Ann, can be found at

FinestOfTheWheat.org/phpgtimeline.

Son Peter shares some of his reminiscences at

FinestOfTheWheat.org/PHPG-Memories.

Recently, a little bird told me that two of Pastor Gutteridge's children are working on a full biography. I wish them every success and hope to be at the front of the line to buy a copy once it is published.

I am grateful to God that I could call this humble servant of Jesus and gifted Bible teacher both "father in the Lord" and friend.

Rev. Jim Kerwin, M.A.
Curator of the works
of Percy Gutteridge

Other Books & Studies from Finest of the Wheat

Titles by Percy Gutteridge
(edited by Jim & Denise Kerwin)

Faith Is Substance
(paperback: https://finestofthewheat.org/faith-paperback; e-book: https://finestofthewheat.org/faith-kindle)

Earth's Most Powerful Preacher (e-book format only)

Our Great Savior God (e-book format only)

The Black Hole (e-book format only)

The Gospel of the Glory (e-book format only)

The Most High and the Elohim (e-book format only)

The Sevenfold Holy Spirit (e-book format only)

This Shall Be a Sign Unto You (e-book format only)

Titles by Jim Kerwin

The Rejected Blessing (available in paperback and e-book formats)

"And Joseph Was Brought Down..." (available in e-book format only)

Circumcision: God's Picture of Sanctification (e-book format only)

Letting In or Getting In? Have We Got the Gospel Backwards? (e-book format only)

That Treasure Trove of Truth (e-book format only)

That Uncomfortable Word—Conviction! (e-book format only)

The "Judicial Adventures" of Paul the Apostle (e-book format only)

The Original Aromas of Christmas (e-book format only)

Who Was the Angel of the LORD? (e-book format only)

Titles by Isaiah Reid

(edited by Jim & Denise Kerwin)

Boyhood Memories and Lessons (available in paperback through FinestOfTheWheat.org/boyhood)

Sunnyside Papers: Inspirational Sketches from God's "Book of Nature" (available in paperback through FinestOfTheWheat.org/sunnyside)

The Holy Way: What It Is, How It Is, and How to Keep It (e-book format only)

Titles by Thomas Cook

(edited by Jim & Denise Kerwin)

New Testament Holiness (e-book format only)